"Cliff, I think we're being a little premature."

Cliff walked up behind Sarah and slipped his arms around her waist. "Oh, in what way?"

"Discussing a commitment."

"Hmm." He nuzzled her ear. "You want to keep this purely sexual. Is that it?"

"No, I mean—I don't know what I mean."

"That's okay." His hands moved upward to cup her breasts. "I'm not the most clearheaded guy in the world right now, either." Gently he stroked her nipples to rigid attention and murmured, "But there's one thing I know for sure...."

"Mmm?"

"The bedroom is that way."

Vicki Lewis Thompson began her writing career at the age of eleven with a short story in the *Auburn Illinois Weekly* and quickly became a byline junkie. Then she discovered she could write books—and she's written a lot of them! In the year 2000, Vicki saw her fiftieth book on the shelves. Vicki lives in Tucson, Arizona, and has two grown children and a husband who encourages her to write from the heart.

VICKI LEWIS THOMPSON

As Time Goes By

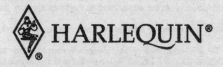

HARLEQUIN®

TORONTO • NEW YORK • LONDON
AMSTERDAM • PARIS • SYDNEY • HAMBURG
STOCKHOLM • ATHENS • TOKYO • MILAN • MADRID
PRAGUE • WARSAW • BUDAPEST • AUCKLAND

To Ruth—
a loving mother-in-law and
a spunky redhead.

ISBN 0-373-63177-4

AS TIME GOES BY

Copyright © 1987 by Vicki Lewis Thompson.

Visit us at www.eHarlequin.com

Printed in U.S.A.

1

DESPITE THE BLOOD, Sarah recognized Cliff immediately.

"Head wound," the paramedic said, locking the gurney wheels. "Got kicked by a horse over at Fort Lowell. Doctor wants a skull series pronto."

"Coming up." Sarah forced herself not to think at all as she maneuvered the X-ray unit into the brightly lit room. Dodging the nurse and taking Cliff's blood pressure, she plugged in the machine and wrestled the heavy armature into position. When her thick red-gold braid fell forward, she flipped it over her shoulder with frowning impatience.

Nothing mattered but focusing the nose of the pale green machine on the left side of Cliff's head, and she thanked the training that allowed her hands to work efficiently while part of her mind remained paralyzed by this sudden confrontation with an injured Cliff Hamilton. Coincidence had never brought someone she knew into the Tucson Medical Center emergency room.

Cliff's muscular body barely fit on the white-sheeted gurney; his Civil War uniform completed the absurd picture. After ten years of no contact, Sarah couldn't believe they'd met again under such bizarre circumstances.

She tried to ignore the blood caked in his wavy brown hair and spattered across both the heavy wool Union fatigue coat and the white cotton shirt underneath. The coat's musty wool scent was out of place, foreign to the sharp, antiseptic smells of the emergency room. Only two of the brass buttons were fastened, as if Cliff had dressed in a hurry.

Sarah lifted troubled brown eyes to the paramedic. "Is he conscious?"

Cliff's warm breath touched her cheek. "Yes, but his head hurts like hell."

At once her gaze dropped to his pale face, and she met the blue eyes she remembered. They were dull, not clear and sparkling with humor as they had been on that long-ago graduation night. Automatically she checked for dilation of his pupils and breathed a sigh of relief when they appeared normal. Recognition flickered in his eyes before he groaned and squeezed his lids shut. "This is going to sound like a line, but believe me, I'm not up to lines right now. Don't I know you?"

He remembered. "Yes, you do, but this is no time for Old Home Week. Lie still."

The paramedic leaning against the wall lifted an eyebrow. "You know this guy?"

"Yes."

"Is he a Hollywood actor?"

"No."

"Then I guess he's an extra. Doesn't it seem funny working on a guy wearing a cavalry uniform? There's another one, the one who rode in the ambulance with us, standing in the waiting room. I keep expecting the Indians to attack."

"All the hostiles have been taken care of," Cliff mumbled. "It's safe to plow your fields."

Sarah glanced quickly at the paramedic. "Has he been babbling like this for long? He could be hallucinating."

Cliff's voice became stronger. "Not a chance, Marvelous Melton."

"Marvelous Melton?" The paramedic grinned.

"Cut it out, Dan." Sarah positioned the film cassette and taped it to the rail of the gurney. "We went to high school together, that's all."

"And she's second only to me in presidential trivia," Cliff added. "I'll show you. Who was Millard Fillmore's wife, Sarah?"

"Abigail Powers," she answered automatically.

"See? She's still got it."

The paramedic shook his head. "Thank God. I've been lying awake nights trying to remember who married old Millard."

"Dan, get lost."

"And miss all the fun?"

"This one's easy, Sarah," Cliff continued. "What was Garfield's middle name?"

"You've got to be quiet, Cliff."

"I will. Just answer that one question."

"Abram," she said with a sigh of exasperation. "I'm going to take the X rays now, and if you move your jaw, all the shots will be screwed up. Don't you have something else to do, Dan?"

The paramedic saluted and stepped toward the door. "I'll go talk to your friend, Mr. Hamilton. He seemed pretty upset. And a guy from the film crew is still hanging around, too."

"Damn. Please tell them both to go back, okay? Pat will miss his chance to be on the silver screen."

"Cliff, that's enough blabbering," Sarah said firmly, preparing for the left lateral shot.

"Yes, ma'am."

He closed his eyes, and he looked so vulnerable and trusting that Sarah had to swallow a very unprofessional pang of tenderness. An extra in a movie—how like the boy she used to know and how different from the conservative real-estate executive he'd become. She wondered if Cliff's father and mother knew about this proposed film debut.

As Sarah straightened Cliff's head on the gurney, her hands cradled his beard-stubbled cheeks. Had she ever touched him? Perhaps she had imagined this so many times that he now felt familiar. Her thumb grazed the soft corner of his mouth. At fifteen she hadn't possessed the experience to imagine kissing Cliff Hamilton.

Sarah had never used her job as an excuse to touch a patient. Never. But this time she allowed the pad of her thumb to move, as if by accident, across the fullness of Cliff's lower lip.

He opened his eyes once to look into her face. "I'm glad you're here, Sarah."

"So am I." And then she remembered her professional position, and the heat rose in her cheeks. "I mean, this is my job. I'm supposed to be here."

"I know. But I'm just...glad." He closed his eyes again and was silent for a moment. "Surprised, though. Isn't some of the work a little gory?"

"Occasionally." She smiled. Cliff didn't realize how bad he looked with blood matted in his thick brown hair.

"You don't seem like the type to..."

"To what?"

"Be here, I guess."

"Well, I am." What did he know about her type? Ten years ago he had been too involved with Julie De-Weese to notice what type she was, except that she was a whiz at presidential trivia.

"You let your hair grow."

"Yes. Be quiet now."

"And it's gotten darker, richer somehow. It used to be almost blond, but now it's sort of like...copper. But you still have those little wispy curls around your face."

"Please be quiet, Cliff." She checked her positioning one last time, then stepped to a cupboard and took out a heavy lead apron. Carefully she placed it over the lower half of Cliff's body.

His eyes flew open. "What's that?"

"A lead apron."

"It's only on half of me."

"That's the half we want to protect." An image of Cliff making love to Julie stuck in her mind. Ten years ago she wouldn't have imagined that, either.

"We do?" Realization dawned in his pain-clouded mind, and he smiled weakly. "Oh. Looking out for future generations of Hamiltons?"

"Doing my job," Sarah said evenly. Damn. First she envisioned Cliff Hamilton's kiss, and now...

"Do you have kids, Sarah?"

"Nope."

"Married?"

"No." Her heart fluttered. Strange he would ask that, unless... No. Her own erotic fantasies were putting ridiculous ideas in her head. "How was Harvard?"

"Fine. How did you know I went there?"

"Your mother. We ran into each other once when she was organizing a fund-raiser for the hospital."

"Yeah, she used to do a lot of those."

"Luckily for TMC. Okay, we've got to stop talking."

"But talking helps me forget my head. Ask me a trivia question."

"In a minute, Cliff. Is the pain really bad?" The misery in his voice reached out to her, and she longed to stroke his forehead in comfort.

"It doesn't tickle."

"I'm sorry," she said helplessly, knowing it was stupid to be apologizing. "Let's get this procedure out of the way so they can get you stitched up."

"Right."

An almost intimate silence filled the room as Sarah snapped the X rays. Her fantasies wouldn't go away. They were no longer the romantic daydreams of a fifteen-year-old. Since then Sarah had progressed through the normal number of dates, steady boyfriends and one ill-fated love affair.

As a boy Cliff had inspired her to scribble countless pages of love notes in her diary. The years had changed them both, and now he prompted cravings that made her blush. But what difference did it make? The outcome would be the same as it had been ten years ago. She and Cliff lived in different worlds.

"I'll have to lift your head a little and put the film under it for the frontal shot," she explained. "I'll be as careful as I can. How old was Teddy Roosevelt when he was inaugurated?"

"Forty-two," Cliff said through gritted teeth.

"How about Van Buren?"

"Uh, let me think. Fifty-four." He held his breath

against the pain as she slipped her hand under his neck and lifted gently. "Damn, but I've got the headache of all headaches going here."

"I know, Cliff. Who was secretary of state under Harrison?"

"Henry Clay. No, Daniel Webster. Hey, remember the time the history club was supposed to watch a film about Second World War naval battles, and Jerry substituted that blue movie?"

"Yes." She'd only vaguely understood the action during the five minutes the film ran before a teacher walked in and ripped it from the projector.

"You were so embarrassed, Sarah."

"I was the only girl in the club."

"I was furious with Jerry for that. Almost ruined our friendship."

"You were furious?"

"He had no right to embarrass you like that."

"But you were laughing, Cliff. I remember."

"Probably. Jerk that I was then, I thought I had to protect my image, when I should have been protecting you."

"I— Thank you, Cliff."

"I always wanted to apologize for that film business."

Always? Sarah wondered if he'd given her even a passing thought in the past ten years. "One more shot and we're done." She clicked the button again. "That should do it. The X rays will be ready in a few minutes, and we'll know whether you're going to be admitted or not."

"Admitted? I don't intend to be admitted." He tried to rise from the gurney.

"Lie flat, please." She placed her hand against his white cotton shirt and pushed him down firmly. She felt the muscles of his chest move under her palm and pulled her hand away quickly as her skin began to tingle. "That uniform's authentic, isn't it?" she asked to cover her agitation.

"That's what Pat tells me. I borrowed it from him." He groaned softly and settled back on the gurney. "Only a history nut would notice. Why aren't you teaching in some stuffy classroom by now, instead of taking pictures of people's insides?"

"Why aren't you, instead of selling people's houses?"

"Believe me, I wish I could be."

Sarah frowned. "You do? Then why—"

"I can't. Not now."

"I don't understand."

"Things have changed, Sarah. Dad has Alzheimer's. I'm needed to run the business."

"Cliff, how terrible! I didn't know that."

"Not many people do so don't tell anyone. Mom's trying to keep it quiet. I guess she doesn't want anybody feeling sorry for him."

Sarah nodded. "I understand. Alzheimer's. That's rough."

"Yeah." They shared a moment of silence, as if to mourn not only the loss of Cliff's father but childhood dreams that now seemed like hopeless fantasies.

"I have to develop the film," Sarah said abruptly, wrenching free of his steady gaze. She sped to the shelter of the darkroom, wanting to be alone with her memories. She could almost smell the chalk dust, hear the scrape of a school desk as Cliff pulled it closer to argue an obscure point of history. They had spent golden afternoons in a deserted classroom discussing how history could be taught, how books could be written so that the study of the past became alive and vital. Their idealistic zeal had made anything seem possible.

Through high school Sarah had clung to the vision of herself as a famous historian, but the scholarship she'd coveted had gone to someone else. Her father's sporadic work in the mines barely put food in eight hungry mouths; he couldn't possibly have financed a liberal arts education for his daughter. Student loans had gotten her through junior college and into this job.

Alone in the darkness, she worked with the strong-smelling chemicals. When the process was complete, she held the finished pieces of celluloid up to the light and mentally crossed her fingers for Cliff's welfare.

"They look clean," she whispered to herself. Hurrying from the darkroom, she jammed the X rays into the clips above the viewer. She scanned the pictures again, then sighed with relief. Cliff was okay. She wasn't qualified to tell him that, of course, but she could carry the X rays downstairs with a light heart, knowing they didn't bring bad news.

Cliff closed his eyes after Sarah had left the emergency room. Because of the pounding in his head, the soft darkness behind his eyelids was preferable to the glare of lights intensified by sterile chrome surfaces. He hadn't meant to tell her about his father. Maybe it was the hospital atmosphere that had made Cliff feel vulnerable, the reminder of all the medical tests that Jack Hamilton had undergone before the final, heartbreaking diagnosis.

Strange that he and Sarah should meet again like this. Whenever he'd thought of Sarah—and it was funny now to realize how many times he *had* thought of her—he pictured her back East teaching history at a women's college or stuck in a rural suburb like Catalina with four children and a miner for a husband.

Either picture made her...unapproachable, and he guessed that was the way he'd wanted it because, every time he thought of Sarah, he was filled with regrets. He regretted never asking her out, never moving outside his social set to discover if he and Sarah had more than a love of history in common. He regretted leaving Canyon del Oro High School without ever really telling her goodbye.

And now she was here, the woman who had peeked out intermittently from the awkward body of a high school sophomore. Gone were the sharp angles and most of the freckles. She had learned to move her five feet eight inches with grace, and he suspected a voluptuous figure lurked under the blue flowered smock and baggy blue pants of her hospital uniform. He smiled. And she still knew her trivia.

Sarah rediscovered was an entrancing experience. Ten years ago she had been so young, so naive, but now... This job she had startled him, though. He wouldn't have expected her to be facing the cruelties of the world every day in a hospital emergency room. Not his shy Sarah. *His?* Where had that come from? Surely he hadn't considered her his, ever. And definitely not after ten years without contact.

But now they had contact, even in the physical sense. What had really jolted him was the touch of her hands on his face, against his mouth. Something had been transmitted with that touch, something he wanted to feel again, in a setting other than this. But probably every patient experienced this emotional connection, he argued with himself. She was in hospital work, and that meant a caring touch, didn't it? It was the same cliché they used in the old war movies—the soldier falls in love with his nurse.

Falls in love. Hey, wait a minute, Hamilton. You only want to have her touch you like that again. Nobody said anything about love. So how can you accomplish getting touched? It's impractical to keep hurting yourself sufficiently to get X rays done all the time.

A cold, wet sponge pressed against the side of his head, and he jerked in reaction. "Sarah?"

"No. I'm Nurse Johnson," a female voice twanged, completely dispelling his tender thoughts. "I'm cleaning you up and shaving some of that hair so we can suture you."

"Where's Sarah?" He sounded like a little kid, but he couldn't help it. Nurse Johnson definitely didn't have Sarah's touch. And the water stung his gashed head.

"She should be back any minute with the X rays. In the meantime, let's take your temperature." Without preamble Nurse Johnson shoved a thermometer in his mouth.

Soon he felt the scraping of a razor against his tortured scalp. "That's a twenty-dollar haircut you're ruining," he muttered around the thermometer.

"Then you shouldn't play horseshoes with it," the nurse said and chuckled at her own joke. Cliff could have wrung her neck. Where in the hell was Sarah? Without her around anything might happen to him.

"Here's the developed film, Dr. Edwards."

Cliff's eyelids flew open at the sound of Sarah's voice across the room. He watched her clip three X rays of his skull to the wall contraption that looked like a hanging light table. The man he assumed was Edwards adjusted his glasses and peered at the film. Sarah glanced at Cliff and smiled. *Oh, Sarah. You have grown up.*

"What took you so long?" Cliff mumbled, shoving the thermometer to one side with his tongue.

"I was only gone a few minutes."

Her sunny expression told him the X rays contained good news. He was fine. He couldn't explain how she said that to him without words, but she did. "Seemed like a few years. Say, Nurse Johnson, do you suppose this thermometer's registered and we can get it out of here?"

"The way you've been jabbering, I doubt it. If you can't stop talking, I can always take your temperature rectally," the nurse replied with smug satisfaction. "The seven-to-three staff is coming on in half an hour, and I don't like to leave any unfinished business when I close up my shift."

Cliff dragged his attention from Sarah to glare at the jowled face of his tormentor. "You try to do that, and you and I will have a lot of unfinished business, Nurse Johnson," he said as distinctly as he could manage around the thermometer. He closed his mouth and looked at Sarah, who was trying not to laugh. Just looking at her made his head hurt less, made his whole world seem brighter.

Dr. Edwards took down the X rays and approached Cliff's gurney. "Well, young man, you're very lucky. No fracture, no concussion. Looks like a nasty cut on the scalp is all you're going to get out of this, although someone should keep an eye on you through the day and tonight. We have to watch for signs of subdural hematoma."

"What?"

"Blood clots, Cliff," Sarah said, coming to his side.

"Can I ride a horse?"

"I wouldn't advise it. Besides, I don't think you're going to feel like charging across the fields after Confederates, or whatever it is you're doing over at Fort Lowell."

Cliff started to explain about the movie, then remembered Nurse Johnson's threat and kept his mouth shut.

"I think the film is more of a Western than a Civil War story," Sarah commented.

Dr. Edwards turned to her, disdain in his voice. "Whatever it is, I get tired of all this idol worship every time Martin Laramour comes to town to shoot another movie." He snorted in disgust. "If we're not careful, Tucson will become another Hollywood."

"But don't you think Laramour's a good director?" Sarah persisted. "His films are historically accurate, but they're also exciting, the way history should be, and—"

"Oh, God." Edwards threw up his hands. "Another Laramour groupie."

Cliff wanted to punch him in his aristocratic nose. How dared he talk to Sarah like that!

"I'm not a groupie," Sarah said quietly. "But I admire Laramour's ability to make history come alive."

Cliff gave her a thumbs-up sign. She was full of surprises. Now she was facing down her boss! Her devotion to history hadn't changed, and he found that reassuring. In fact, everything about her was reassuring. A sort of warm homecoming.

Dr. Edwards favored Sarah with a patronizing smile. "Sounds like you ought to be one of Laramour's extras, too."

"Perhaps," Sarah replied without blinking.

Inspiration flashed through Cliff's numbed brain. Of course! What a terrific idea. When Nurse Johnson pulled the thermometer from his mouth, he jumped into the conversation. "Why don't you come with me to the park for the day, Sarah? You'd love it."

"Uh, Cliff, I..." She hesitated, guessing what Edwards might think. How many times had he lectured her about making dates with emergency room patients?

Judging from Sarah's hesitation and the two grooves between Edwards's eyebrows, Cliff sensed he'd broached a touchy subject, and although he found himself bristling at the man's proprietary air, he didn't want Sarah to get into trouble because of him. "Let me explain, Dr. Edwards. Sarah and I have known each other since high school. In fact, we were in the history club together."

"Oh. I see." His tone could have frozen a Florida swamp.

"I don't think I can make it today, anyway, Cliff. But thanks for asking."

Silently Cliff cursed his impetuousness. If he'd asked

her in private, he wouldn't have put her professionalism on the line and she might have accepted.

Edwards handed the X rays to Sarah. "If you'll file these, we'll get this gentleman sewn up and on his way."

To Sarah the implication was clear. *Let's get back to work and forget about fraternizing with the patients.* "I'll tell Nurse Johnson you're ready to suture, Dr. Edwards," she said, not looking at Cliff as she accepted the X rays.

"While you're doing that, I'll let Mr. Hamilton's friend know the injury isn't serious." The doctor walked briskly into the waiting room.

Cliff groaned to himself. Battle-ax Johnson was about to replace his precious Sarah, and he knew the next few minutes would not be pleasant.

Sarah filed the X rays and glanced at the clock. Fifteen minutes more of her shift and she had the weekend to herself. Whoopee. Another wild two days spent feeding her goldfish, Mabel and Manfred. Too bad she couldn't have gone to Fort Lowell with Cliff. She'd like to hear more about his father. Poor Cliff—he'd always had everything, and now...

But he'd picked the wrong time to ask her. She couldn't afford to alienate Edwards and possibly even jeopardize her job.

Besides, any involvement with Cliff Hamilton was a no-future situation if she'd ever seen one. The gulf yawning between them made the Grand Canyon look

like a tiny ditch. What would a Harvard graduate who
was a full partner in his father's real-estate firm have in
common with an X-ray technician who barely paid her
bills each month?

An orderly pushed a wheelchair into the emergency
room, and Sarah paused in her record-keeping chores
to see if Cliff had opted for the wheelchair. Probably
not, if Cliff Hamilton the man was anything like Cliff
Hamilton the boy. Hadn't she once seen him limp off
the football field, then charge back on two plays later?
Sure enough, he came staggering out of the emergency
room, looking pale but determined.

Dr. Edwards followed, a look of exasperation on his
patrician face. "Your friend said he'd come back in an
hour or so, Hamilton. Why don't you sit in the waiting
room until he gets here?"

"No. I'll be fine. Just fine." He swayed slightly and
gripped the counter surrounding the nurses' station.

"Well, I can't recommend this plan of yours to walk
back to the park alone. You should be driven home."

Cliff closed his eyes briefly, then looked directly at
the doctor. "I'm not going home. I'm going back to the
park." He managed a wry smile. "A slight injury like
this won't stop a Laramour groupie."

Sarah wanted to hug him, especially after she wit-
nessed with satisfaction the flush on Edwards's face.

"Whatever you decide to do, then," the doctor said
crisply, "my responsibility is over."

Sarah moved forward involuntarily, suddenly afraid

for Cliff's safety. "You really can't walk over there by yourself, you know."

"Why not?" The challenge in his blue eyes reminded her of their debates of long ago.

She shook her head impatiently. "It's not wise. Somebody needs to be with you to watch you for signs of a blood clot."

"What are the signs?"

Dr. Edwards stepped up to the counter and picked up a stack of files. "Projectile vomiting, for one," he said matter-of-factly.

Cliff's face turned a shade paler. "Does that mean what I think it does?"

Edwards nodded. "Probably. Still want to risk it for the sake of Martin Laramour?"

Cliff hesitated, then glanced at the clock. "Isn't your shift nearly over, Sarah?"

"Yes."

"If it wouldn't be too much trouble, maybe you could give me a ride to the park." He turned to her and lifted his eyebrows. "I'll sit in the waiting room until you're ready to go."

She could see no graceful way out of this, and concern for Cliff's well-being overrode her nervousness about displeasing Edwards. Ever since she'd begun working at TMC, he'd warned her about turning the emergency room into a place to find dates, almost as if he assumed she'd taken the job for just that purpose.

Damn it, she had a right to see Cliff safely to the park without being branded a man hunter!

"I'll give you a ride on my way home, Cliff. It's in the same direction." She glanced at Edwards, and he nodded curtly, like a father giving permission. Boiling inside, she managed a thin smile.

"Thanks, Sarah," Cliff said, his voice weak. "I'll be in the waiting room."

"Let me help." She started toward him.

"No, no." He held up one hand. "I can do it. I'll just take it slow."

Sarah watched anxiously until he sank onto the plastic cushions of a waiting-room chair. "I'll just be a minute," she called over her shoulder as she headed upstairs to change. Moments later she was back, her hospital scrubs replaced by jeans and a sea-green knit polo shirt.

Cliff didn't look good. He was slumped in the chair, his eyes closed and his skin blanched nearly as white as the square of gauze taped to the side of his head. As she moved closer, Sarah groped in her shoulder purse for her keys. Perhaps she should insist he go home after all. She could take him there, and he could pick up his car later.

As if he felt her watching him, his eyes opened, and he smiled. "Hi."

"Hi, yourself. Do you feel up to leaving?"

"I think so." As he sat up straighter, he took in her

total appearance. "You're not nearly as scrawny as you used to be, Sarah."

"Thanks, I think." She smiled. No flowery praises, but his eyes *had* opened a little wider, and his gaze had lingered, ever so slightly, on her womanly curves.

"You're welcome." Cliff closed his eyes as a wave of pain took him by surprise.

"I think I should take you home, Cliff." She paused, reluctant to pry into his private life. "Is there someone who could care for you there?"

"Afraid not. I live alone."

"Oh." She reprimanded herself for enjoying that news. "Well, I'm worried that the filming may be too much for you today."

"Not if you stay with me." He rose unsteadily to his feet and glanced around. "And speaking of Edwards, he's not around now so you're free to say yes; if you'd like to spend the day together. Just like old times, Sarah. How about it?"

She thought about it for only a second longer. "I'd love to."

2

"TERRIFIC."

Cliff's grateful smile made her warm with happiness. Maybe too much happiness. Just because he needed her today didn't mean anything. They'd catch up on each other's lives and part because they still existed in two separate worlds.

They walked together through the automatic doors, and the cool spring air brushed Sarah's skin. She lifted her face to welcome the sunshine after eight hours under fluorescent lights.

Cliff took a deep breath. "Sure smells good out here compared to the antiseptic. I think that was part of what made me dizzy."

"Maybe. But a hundred and twenty years ago, without that modern care, you would have been in a world of trouble."

"True. I wouldn't want to go back in time, but pretending for the weekend is fun. Pat, my friend from Phoenix who got me into this movie thing, spends almost all his weekends reenacting Civil War stuff with other members of his historical club, F Troop. I can't decide if he's dedicated or nuts."

"Sounds like fun to me."

"To me, too," Cliff admitted. "Maybe I'm jealous because I can't spare that many weekends to play around."

"Cliff...this situation with your father...it really changed things, didn't it?"

"Sure did. But he can't help it, poor guy. Which car is yours?"

She pointed to a red Volkswagen. "Over there."

"I see it."

As they approached the brightly colored, economy bug, Sarah wondered what sort of luxury car Cliff drove now. She remembered his burgundy Corvette in high school and how the color had complemented Julie DeWeese's raven hair.

While she searched for her keys, Cliff relaxed with a sigh against the sun-warmed fender.

"Hope you can squeeze in," she said, opening the passenger's door. "I'm a little short on leg room."

"That's okay. You're a pal to help me out, Sarah. If the encampment's no fun, I promise to buy you dinner next weekend to make up for it."

"That's not necessary." Her heart took an unexpected skip at his casual mention of another date, and she scurried around to the driver's side.

"Don't speak too soon. Maureen and Pat have insisted on making this encampment authentic so you'll have to eat whatever stuff they've brought."

"Couldn't be worse than the leftovers in my refrigerator." Banter was the key, she decided. But as she slid behind the steering wheel, she realized just how small the car's interior really was.

"You live by yourself?"

So much for banter. Cliff wasn't keeping any physical or emotional distance between them. "Except for Mabel and Manfred."

"Who are?"

"Barracuda posing as goldfish. Voracious eaters. It's all I can do to keep them in shrimp flakes."

"I'd like to meet them sometime."

"Sure." Meet her goldfish? Was that a hint to be invited to her apartment? This wasn't going at all as she had expected. Her hand shook as she fitted the key in the ignition.

"Sarah, you're trembling. What's the matter?"

"Too much coffee, I guess." She started the engine and put the car in Reverse.

"Do you drink a lot of coffee?"

"No."

"Then what's wrong?"

Sarah braked to a stop at the parking-lot exit and took a deep breath. "Maybe I'd better not spend the day with you, Cliff."

"Why not?"

"I might do something stupid. Suddenly I feel fifteen again. Surely you realized I had a megacrush on you in high school. I don't want to make either of us uncomfortable."

He was silent for several seconds. "Megacrush? Really?"

"Don't tell me you didn't know it. I was so obvious, I'm sure."

"No, Sarah. I didn't know it. I wish I had."

"Don't be silly, Cliff. If you'd known, it wouldn't have made a difference. Don't you remember what I looked like back then? Freckles, ostrich legs, the general fifteen-year-old blahs. When I stacked myself up against Julie DeWeese, I gave myself five-thousand-to-one odds."

"You weren't that bad."

"I was, too. You're just being gallant."

He chuckled softly. "No, I'm not. I distinctly remember thinking you had a very nice pair of—"

"Cliff!"

"Big brown eyes. Ha! Gotcha."

She colored furiously. "See? I'm not in your league, Cliff. Never have been. I'll drive you over there, and one of your buddies can watch over you today. If you like, I'll even tell them what to look for."

"Don't do it, Sarah," he said quietly.

"Don't do what?"

"Slam the door on me, right when I'm thanking my lucky stars that horse kicked me in the head so I could find you again. We were friends once." He paused. "I'd like to be friends again. Lord knows, I could use a friend these days."

She glanced at him. "It's that bad?"

"You work in a hospital. You've seen people with Alzheimer's."

Sarah let out her breath slowly. "Yes."

"When Pat called offering a chance to live in a fantasy world for the weekend, I jumped at it. Having you there, a wonderful reminder of the past, would make it perfect. Please, Sarah."

She glanced at him, then averted her gaze, afraid he would see the emotion threatening to spill over. "All right," she said softly, resting her chin on the steering wheel. After a quiet moment she straightened and put the car in gear. "I guess Manfred and Mabel can do without me for one day."

"That's the spirit, Sarah."

"But I can only spend one day."

"If you say so."

As THEY NEARED THE PARK, a single rider in a navy-blue coat like Cliff's mounted his horse and cantered up the wide lane of the cottonwoods while ahead of him a truck fitted with camera equipment filmed his ride. A man with a mop of gray hair stood behind the cameraman, and Sarah wondered if he could be Laramour.

Fort Lowell Park had been altered to resemble the army post it had once been. Picnic ramadas had been transformed into barracks, and a man armed with a clipboard and a bullhorn ambled between two rows of khaki tents facing each other. Across a large field, near the ruins of the original Fort Lowell, Sarah could see trailers and more camera equipment. Small groups of soldiers and a cluster of women in long dresses talked idly, awaiting their turn before the lens.

"The filming's begun," Cliff said as Sarah parked the car next to the curb. He glanced at a gold chain dangling from a small pocket below the waistband of her jeans. "Wouldn't happen to have the time, would you?"

Without thinking, Sarah pulled out her great-grandfather's pocket watch and snapped open the case. "Seven-thirty."

Cliff smiled triumphantly. "I was right. You're carrying that watch. Boy, does it bring back memories."

"You remember this watch?"

"You bet. It caused our only big fight. You brought it to show everyone in the history club, and I offered to buy it."

"I'm amazed you remember. I'm sure I was very rude."

"No. I was rude to place monetary value on an heirloom. But I wanted that watch. My family hasn't handed down much of anything."

"The watch means a lot to me," Sarah admitted, holding the gold timepiece in the palm of her hand. "My parents gave it to me for high school graduation. For a while I kept it in a bell jar in my apartment, but last year I started carrying it whenever I was wearing jeans with the right kind of pocket."

"Good for you." Admiration shone in his blue eyes,

and she grew increasingly warm in the glow of emotion. Cliff leaned forward slightly, and Sarah had the distinct impression he might kiss her.

Abruptly she snapped the case shut and changed the subject. "Which horse kicked you?" She waved at the string of docile-looking animals tethered to a rope stretched between two trees. "They don't look very wild to me."

Cliff smiled at her deliberate maneuver. Okay. She wasn't ready. "That big bay gelding on the end, and it wasn't his fault. We were both trying to kill the same rattlesnake, and we got in each other's way."

"Rattlesnake?" In spite of all her years in the desert, Sarah felt a thrill of fear at the thought of a rattler. "Are you sure it wasn't some old gopher snake, Cliff?"

"I'm sure. But if you don't believe me, I imagine the boys kept the carcass around here somewhere. It may be in somebody's stewpot by now."

"Yuck!" She eyed the smoking campfires with suspicion.

"Why not? That's what the soldiers did in the 1860s." He grinned at her. "Don't worry. I'm sure they had finicky eaters in those days, too."

"I am not finicky! I just don't like snakes."

"Okay. How about snails?"

"You've got to be kidding."

"Frogs' legs?"

"Not on your life." She leaned against the car door and turned to face him, ready to put the distance of their backgrounds between them. "Those are gourmet foods, Cliff, which I've never considered eating because I couldn't afford them. You know, except for an interest in history, I bet we don't have a single thing in common."

He looked at her thoughtfully. "I wouldn't say that."

"Then name something."

"Both of us are still searching for what we want from life." He surprised himself by saying that. He couldn't remember ever having thought about his future in those terms, but now that he'd said the words, he recognized the ring of truth. Had he guessed correctly about her?

"I suppose." She allowed herself to meet the clear blue of his eyes for a moment and thought she saw a flicker of anticipation, making her heart race. Afraid he would find his words confirmed by her expression, she turned away. "Let's get you out and see how you are at walking around now," she said briskly.

She reached the passenger's side of the car before Cliff finished extricating his long legs from under the dashboard, and she stretched out both hands. "Let me help you, Cliff," she said as he started to rise. "If you stand up too fast, you're liable to crumple."

He rested his palms on hers. As she took both of his hands, her tingling senses recorded everything with the accuracy of a video tape machine. Would she play back these moments for the rest of her life? "On the count of three, you stand up, and I'll help support you. One, two, three."

Slowly he stood, then swayed gently forward. "Sarah, I think I—" he mumbled just before she dropped his hands and slipped her hands under his armpits to stop him from falling. He slumped against her, and his arms folded automatically around her waist.

She stiffened in concern. "Damn, I was afraid of this. Are you sure I shouldn't take you home?" she muttered against the rough wool of his jacket. She struggled to hold him upright as his broad chest crushed her breasts. But, oh, the excitement of holding him close!

"No, no. Just give me a minute," Cliff muttered, his cheek resting on top of her hair as the spinning sensation subsided. She felt terrific. She smelled terrific. Someday he might hate himself for being so weak in front of her, but at this moment the pressure of her body against him was worth the loss of his macho image.

As warm desire flowed through her, Sarah realized she had to break the intimate contact, and soon. "Do you think you can stand alone yet?" she pleaded against his chest. "My arms are about ready to give out."

"Let me see." Slowly he straightened, moving away from her with reluctance. "That's better," he said, taking a deep breath. He felt immeasurably better as he looked into her soft brown eyes. "I won't pretend that

didn't feel mighty nice, Sarah. You're so soft and—
Damn, here comes Pat."

Just as well. Sarah tried to control her trembling. She
wouldn't have wanted to hear whatever Cliff had been
about to say, anyway. Not unless she wanted her heart
broken a second time.

"Hey, Cliff!" called a man with a full black beard. "I
just realized it was you over here. You should have
waited until I came to get you."

"Sarah offered to bring me to the park. Pat Murphey,
I'd like you to meet Sarah Melton, most recently my
X-ray technician for this head thing, but ten years ago a
high school friend."

"You work at TMC?" Pat grasped her hand.

"Good luck for me, I can tell you," Cliff said. "She
pulled me through that ordeal in fine shape, but you
should get a load of Nurse Johnson, Pat. Uglier than a
javelina and twice as mean."

"Cliff! Madge Johnson is not—" Sarah started to
laugh, remembering the times she'd made a similar
private assessment.

"Anyway, you got back safely." Pat threw an arm
around Cliff's shoulders. "How's the head?"

"Surface wound, apparently."

"Hey, that's great. Still up to playing soldier for Laramour?"

Cliff glanced at Sarah. "On a limited basis. I brought
along my nurse. I also expected Laramour would take

one look at her gorgeous red hair and rope her into the filming, too."

Pat laughed. "Gorgeous red hair is always in demand on a movie set, I understand. Care to join us, Sarah?"

"Be in the movie?"

"Sure. Might as well get paid while you're helping Cliff. It isn't a lot, but some spare change never hurts."

"You're right. If Laramour can use me, I'd be a fool not to take the job."

Cliff glanced at her. "Laramour would be a fool not to hire you."

"You're making her blush, Cliff."

"I know. I think she looks great when she blushes."

Sarah rushed to change the subject before she turned beet red. "I don't have anything to wear, though. Does Laramour have costumes, Pat?"

"Probably, but my wife can loan you something. Why not go into the casting office already decked out? They'll love it. Laramour may want to trade you for this character." He grinned good-naturedly at Cliff. "He's turning out to be more trouble than he's worth."

Cliff snorted. "Some gratitude, Murphey."

"Just practical. If the snake had bitten a horse, we could have shot the horse. But you're injured, and we have to patch you up. Takes more time."

"I'll remember that next time, Captain, sir." Cliff gave a ragged salute.

Pat guffawed, then studied his friend for a moment.

"You sure you're going to be feeling well enough to participate this weekend?"

"Wouldn't miss it. I may not be able to ride in the charges, but with Sarah here to watch over me, I can at least get in on some general crowd scenes. I'll be careful, Pat."

"Sure you will, Hamilton. And Tucson will get snow this afternoon. I'll find Maureen and ask about the dresses." Pat left in search of his wife, leaving Sarah and Cliff alone again.

"Sorry if I embarrassed you, Sarah. But you look so pretty when your cheeks get pink. I remember noticing that after the blue-movie episode."

"And I haven't changed a bit, as you see."

"I wouldn't say that. In fact, you intrigue the hell out of me, Sarah Jane."

"I do?"

"Uh-huh." He touched her cheek with his knuckles. "Very much."

"Oh." Sarah looked into his blue eyes and absorbed his caress with every nerve in her body. Her breathing became shallow, and she knew that, if he tried to kiss her now, she wouldn't stop him. He smiled, acknowledging the lowering of a barrier, and then someone spoke beside them.

"Sarah? I'm Maureen."

Sarah glanced around and met green eyes fringed by startling black lashes. Clouds of dark hair surrounded a milk-white complexion, and Sarah decided Maureen was a good name for someone so definitely Irish. "I'm glad to meet you," she said, taking the other woman's outstretched hand. "Pat said you might be able to—"

"No problem. When Laramour called Pat and asked if F Troop would like to be part of the film, I packed every dress I had! Come on over to the camper, and I'll show you some."

"Okay. I'll—I'll see you later, Cliff."

His blue gaze held her brown one for a split second. "You bet," he said, and she wished her heart wouldn't thump like a jackrabbit's at such a simple answer. "And Sarah?"

She paused in the act of turning away. "Yes?"

"I wish you'd take your hair out of the braid."

"Uh, we'll see." Not daring to look at him again, Sarah walked beside Maureen to the camper. She felt Cliff's attention still on her, and before following Maureen through the tiny back doorway, she peeked over her shoulder. Sure enough, he was standing in exactly the same spot, staring after them. Sarah waved timidly, and Cliff raised one hand to his lips to blow her a kiss. Heat flooded her body as she hastily stumbled inside the camper and slammed the door.

"Pat says you knew Cliff in high school." Maureen shook the folds from a chocolate-brown dress with white lace trim. She laid the dress on a small bed and reached for a pale green gown with tiny blue flowers sprinkled across it.

"I was a sophomore when he was a senior. These

dresses are beautiful, Maureen. Where did you find something so perfect?"

"I sew. I also made Pat's uniform and some of the other men's clothes, too."

"Sounds like a lot of work for a hobby."

Maureen laughed. "Don't let Pat hear you call it a hobby. He takes F Troop very seriously. I sometimes wonder if the real frontier soldiers worked as hard as these guys do pretending to be frontier soldiers."

"I didn't mean to belittle what they do. I think it's a fascinating way to relive history, but between making uniforms and spending your weekends camping out and reenacting battles, you must devote all your spare time to F Troop."

"Just about. But if you love history the way we do, it beats playing cards."

"I'm sure it does." Sarah stroked the soft cotton of the green dress. "I once planned to teach history."

"Did you? What made you change your mind?"

"I didn't really change it, I just...got into something else," Sarah finished lamely. "But I'm looking forward to a whole day with a bunch of history buffs."

"I think you'll have fun. Cliff's a terrific guy. With a tough row to hoe."

"You mean his father."

Maureen nodded. "We hoped this weekend might take his mind off his problems. And if I believed in fate, I'd think the accident was planned so he could meet you again."

"We were just buddies in high school, Maureen. We aren't long-lost sweethearts or anything."

"Could've fooled me."

Sarah realized Maureen was referring to the scene she'd interrupted a moment ago. The dark-haired woman was probably bursting with questions she dared not ask, and Sarah dared not answer.

"May I try these on?" she said to fill the awkward silence.

"Of course. I'll step outside so you can have some privacy."

When the camper door closed, Sarah sat on the bed. Should she leave now, before Cliff got a tighter grip on her heart? And his well-meaning friends seemed to think a romance was in the offing. They couldn't know how impossible that was, considering Cliff's high-rolling life-style. She would never fit in.

She ran an appreciative hand over Maureen's dresses, longing to put one on, wanting to look attractive for Cliff. She could at least try one.

Quickly she stripped to her bra and panties and reached for the green-and-blue dress because it buttoned up the front. The brown one had a row of tiny pearl buttons up the back; she'd never be able to get it on without help.

Except for a little tightness in the bust, the dress fit perfectly. Sarah had no mirror, but she could tell from glancing down that the scoop-necked bodice, which may have been quite modest on Maureen, looked a tad wicked on her. Then she spied her feet and started to giggle. The jogging shoes would have to go. Did Maureen have antique shoes, too?

She started to open the door to find Maureen, but she paused with one hand on the doorknob. Then she flipped her braid over her shoulder and unwound the rubber band that held the ends of her red-gold hair. She rummaged in her purse for a small brush, tilted her head to one side and stroked vigorously. Moments later her hair was falling around her shoulders and halfway down her back in rippling waves. Taking a deep breath, she reached once more for the doorknob.

Several yards away a pair of blue eyes watched the closed camper door. Slowly Cliff sipped his coffee from a tin mug and tried to listen as Pat and Martin Laramour discussed the strategy for the remainder of the day's filming. He registered their conversation, but his attention was trained on that door. Asking her to take her hair down had been an afterthought, but he was glad he had. If she granted his request, they were making progress. He had no trouble picturing what she'd look like when she took it out of the confining braid, and he longed to slide his fingers through the copper waves.

But her hair wasn't all he wanted to touch. Every inch of her body beckoned him with an intensity that amazed him. He grew weak from imagining his hands stroking the fullness of her breasts, the silken length of her thighs, the— He shut his eyes against the sensations building inside him. And she was afraid of him, apparently because of his money and social position.

"And you might be able to help load the wounded on the wagon after the battle, Cliff," Pat said. "Cliff? Are you listening?"

"What?"

The men sitting around the fire laughed. "I think Cliff's mind is on other matters," teased a tall man with wire-rimmed glasses. "Maybe we'd better put him in charge of guarding the women."

"That would be fine," Cliff said absently, and the men exchanged winks as he returned his gaze to the camper door.

"Think you'll be able to keep your mind on the filming, Hamilton?" Laramour asked, a sparkle of humor in his brown eyes. "Pretend love is great on the screen, but real love can louse up the schedule."

Cliff opened his mouth to protest. Love? He might be a little preoccupied, but...

"Leave him alone," Pat said, coming to his rescue. "I remember feeling that way about Maureen at the beginning, although you turkeys may never have been lucky enough to find someone who inspired that dazed expression on Cliff's face."

At that moment the camper door swung open, and Cliff's jaw dropped. Sarah raised the hem of her skirt to reveal slim ankles and bare feet as she climbed down the camper steps.

"What's the matter, haven't you ever seen a woman

in a dress, Hamilton?" Pat joked, poking Cliff in the ribs.

"Not looking like that," Cliff answered without thinking. She'd taken her hair down, just as he'd asked, and in the process had given herself an air of vulnerability and muted passion that spoke of another age, a time when a man defended a woman's honor with a sharp blade and a strong arm. Cliff felt an overwhelming need to be the man who protected Sarah from all calamities.

"I can see what you mean," commented the man in the wire-rimmed glasses. "That dress fits real good in the top."

Cliff's newfound role as protector sharpened his tongue. "Keep your comments to yourself, Bill. Excuse me, gentlemen." Cliff got up to his feet and hurried to the camper as the other men exchanged knowing glances.

From the corner of her eye, Sarah saw Cliff approaching as she gingerly made her way across the sparse grass to the picnic table where Maureen was measuring flour into a bowl. Sarah pretended not to notice him.

"What do you think?" she asked Maureen as she reached the table and put down her bundle containing her own clothes, her grandfather's watch and her purse.

Maureen glanced up from the biscuits she was shaping and blinked. "Wow. You fill out that dress much better than I do, Sarah. After seeing how you look in it, I may not have the nerve to wear it again. Wouldn't care to buy it, would you?"

"Well, I..." Sarah hesitated, remembering her meager salary and her precious savings account. And she'd never have another reason to wear the dress.

"Let me buy it for you, Sarah."

Sarah's head swiveled slowly toward Cliff, and her heart leaped at the tenderness she read in his face. "Cliff, I really couldn't accept—"

"I wish you would." Cliff's blue-eyed gaze roved over her wistfully. "The dress is perfect for you."

"But you can't justify buying something to wear once, Cliff."

"I can afford it."

"That's not the point." But it was. His willingness to buy the dress on an impulse, when she had to hoard every penny she earned, bothered her. "You don't pay for a dress you'll wear once. That's wasteful, no matter how much money you have."

"You're talking nonsense."

"Only from your point of view, Cliff. We look at everything from different angles." She glanced regretfully into his blue eyes. "You see, we're disagreeing already. Maybe my staying here is a mistake. Perhaps I'd better go home."

3

"Excuse us a minute, Maureen." Cliff cupped Sarah's elbow and guided her toward a spot out of earshot of Maureen and the cavalry group. "Watch your bare feet, Sarah. The grass is full of goathead stickers."

"I understand about goathead stickers, Cliff. My parents deal with them all the time in Catalina. They live in a double-wide trailer out there."

"I know you're from Catalina."

"Cliff, don't you see? We were miles apart in high school, and it's still the same. Our backgrounds are totally different."

"So this is about money."

"Not only money. Social position, and education, and all the life experiences that separate us. It's best if I go home, and we'll forget we ran into each other."

He moved a step closer and ran gentle fingers along the side of her neck. "I'm afraid I can't do that." His eyes were the warmest blue she'd ever seen, and his smile could undermine the strongest resolve. "I think we can solve our problems, Sarah. Give it time."

She drew a quivering breath as the feather touch of his fingers played havoc with her logic. "But, Cliff, when one person is rich, and the other is...not, the person who isn't often feels...at a disadvantage."

He studied her for a moment. "Okay. I'll accept that. Why did you decide to spend the day with me, then?"

"It sounded like fun. Besides, after you mentioned your father's illness, I believed I could—" she shrugged "—help somehow, although that seems silly."

"No, it's not silly. I haven't told many people exactly what's wrong with Dad. But I told you. Just like I used to cry on your shoulder in high school."

"Sarah, the official wailing wall."

He grimaced. "Sounds like I used you, doesn't it? And maybe that's what happened before I was old enough to know any better. But I'm not a kid anymore, Sarah. I've learned to give as well as take."

"As in dresses?"

"You know that's not what I mean."

"I know. But I really can't accept the dress, Cliff."

"You're sure?"

She nodded.

"Okay. Too bad, though." He picked up a lock of her copper hair and drew it across her shoulder to nestle against the neckline of her dress. "There. You look just like an officer's wife in one of the old Fort Lowell photographs. Seems a shame you'll never wear that dress again."

The whisper of his fingers in her hair and against her skin wiped out the last of her reason and determination, and she wished for something, or someone, to lean against.

"You know," he continued in the same low, coaxing tone, "you have the perfect face for those old pictures. High forehead, eyes set wide apart..." He traced her lips with the tip of a finger. "And a full mouth that begs for a man's kisses."

She listened in dazed compliance. She didn't stand a chance.

His finger left her lips and slid under her chin to tilt her face up to his. "You could turn a man's head, Sarah."

His gaze drifted to her mouth, and she knew in the space of another heartbeat he would kiss her, and all would be lost. This wasn't going at all the way she'd planned it.

"No." She shook her head.

"Yes."

She watched, hypnotized, as he bent toward her. "Cliff, this is a mis—"

Ignoring her words, he began a leisurely exploration of her lips. With gentle pressure on her chin, he urged her mouth open, muffling her protest with a deeper kiss.

Her hands flattened against the rough wool of his jacket. As his tongue dipped into her mouth, she could feel his heartbeat quicken under the thick material. The pace of her heart matched his, and she fought to keep from wrapping her arms around his neck and pulling him closer.

Gathering what little strength remained, she braced both hands against his chest. The brass buttons imprinted themselves on her palms as she pushed herself free, and his head jerked with the force of her shove. He groaned, and her eyes widened in horror when he staggered backward, holding his head in both hands.

"Cliff!" She rushed to him and grasped his shoulders. "Cliff, I'm sorry! Are you okay?" She peered into his pale face. "I forgot, Cliff. I shouldn't have—"

"No, you sure as hell shouldn't." He opened his eyes slowly and managed a weak grin while something akin to the *1812 Overture* played loudly in his head. "Not after decking yourself out in that dress and wearing your hair down for me."

She dropped her gaze, her brown eyes dark with guilt. "You're right. I did."

"One look at you in that dress, with your hair down, and I was ready to kneel at your feet, Sarah."

"Thanks to me, you almost fell at my feet," she said unhappily.

"I'll be okay. I guess we're even now." He cupped her face in his hands. "I won't try that again until I'm sure you won't push me away."

"I feel like a fool, Cliff."

"Don't. I shouldn't have rushed you. Come on, let's go back to the others."

He took her hand in a loose, companionable grip,

and tears misted Sarah's eyes. Damn it, he really was a terrific guy who didn't deserve such shabby treatment. His sudden appearance in her life and his obvious interest had thrown her into total confusion. She was giving off contradictory signals, and the poor man didn't know which response she wanted. Trouble was, neither did she.

The bark of the bullhorn interrupted her thoughts. "Cavalry gather for Indian raid sequence," came the curt order.

"Over here, Cliff!" Pat called from the row of tents.

"You shouldn't go." She clutched his hand in alarm.

He glanced down at her and smiled. "Worried?"

"Of course I am! Indian raids don't sound like your average crowd scene to me. I picture mayhem, screaming, widespread shedding of blood, things like that."

"And all make-believe," Cliff assured her, already backing in the direction of the tents. "I'll be careful." As the distance increased between them, he raised his voice. "Don't worry. I'll come back to you, Sarah Jane." Then, after an exaggerated salute, he strode toward the tents.

"Sarah!" Maureen's voice drifted across the clearing.

Sarah turned and saw several women clustered by the picnic table where Maureen had been making biscuits.

"Come on over here," Maureen called. "We're not in this scene so you may as well join us for coffee."

As Sarah hobbled toward the table, rocks and goathead stickers bit into her bare feet. Funny, she hadn't noticed them when she'd walked the same path with Cliff.

"I didn't think about shoes." Maureen handed her a steaming tin cup. "I'll be glad to loan you some, if you can wear a size seven."

"I can probably squeeze into them." Sarah sipped the hot liquid, glad to have something to do besides thinking of Cliff in the middle of a battle scene. "I really appreciate your generosity, Maureen. I—I convinced Cliff not to buy the dress for me, after all."

"Oh. Well, that's fine." The flicker of hurt in Maureen's green eyes was quickly countered by a brilliant smile. "Shall we watch the action? The Apaches are amassing across the field."

"I don't know if I can watch. Cliff shouldn't be doing this, not so soon after leaving the emergency room."

"Pat just handed him a rifle so I think it's out of our hands."

Sarah followed the direction of Maureen's gaze and watched as the man with the clipboard explained the scene to the group of soldiers. Her blood chilled. What if Cliff tripped and fell? The camera crew moved into position, and the band of Apaches kicked their horses into a gallop, straight for the row of tents.

"He shouldn't be doing this, Maureen," she repeated, gripping her new friend's arm.

"You're probably right, but how do you propose to stop him? The Cliff Hamilton I know isn't easily led."

"He's not, but it's for his own—oh! He's—he's fallen to the ground!" With a cry she gathered her skirts high and raced toward him, unmindful of her tender feet. Her red-gold hair streamed in the wind, and her bare legs flew as she ran toward Cliff's body sprawled in the dust.

"Cliff! Say something." She knelt next to his crumpled form. He had fallen on his right side, and she thanked whatever luck had kept him from landing on his bandaged head. "Are you all right? Talk to me!"

"Cut!" yelled a voice.

"Cliff!" she persisted. "Say something!"

Slowly he rolled over and eyed her balefully. "Sarah, I was supposed to be dead here."

"What do you mean, dead?"

"I got shot at close range, and I had to fall down and pretend deadness. Haven't you ever played cowboys and Indians, Sarah?"

"You mean you *intended* to fall down?"

"Yep."

"Cliff Hamilton, I could strangle you."

"That would make my situation more realistic, which it certainly isn't anymore."

Gradually Sarah became aware of her surroundings, of the soldiers milling around her, of the painted faces of the Indian actors as they reined in their horses and, last, of the man with the clipboard standing directly beside her. He didn't look pleased.

"Are you with the company, ma'am?" he asked with feigned politeness.

"Yes, she is," said Cliff before Sarah could deny it.

"Then find the schedule of scenes and memorize it, please. We've got a movie to make."

"Uh, certainly." Sarah stood up and brushed the dust from her skirt before looking the man straight in the eye. "But I suggest you think twice before you tell this man to fall down. He has a head injury."

"Don't blame me, ma'am. He volunteered to be one of the ones killed."

"He *what*?" Sarah's fists went to her hips as she faced Cliff, who was getting to his feet. "You must be out of your—"

Cliff straightened his jacket. "I knew what I was doing, Sarah. After all, I wasn't on a horse, was I? It's all anticipation and knowing when to fall. When you pushed me before, I wasn't expecting it." He adjusted his cap and grinned at her. "I'm honored that you were so worried about me. It's nice to know someone will come running when you're down and out."

Sarah's nails bit into the palms of her hands as she fought to contain her anger and embarrassment. "Just remember the little boy who called *wolf*," she said through clenched teeth. Then, swirling her skirts around her, she stalked back toward the picnic table where Maureen and the other women waited.

A wistful smile curved Cliff's mouth as he watched

her go. "At least I know you care a little," he said under his breath.

Maureen came to meet her. "Is he all right?"

"He's terrific," Sarah muttered. "Terrifically stubborn, terrifically boneheaded, terrifically smug..."

Maureen laughed. "I've had those same thoughts about Pat. Come and help me finish breakfast. Everybody'll want something to eat when the scene's been shot."

"Uh, Maureen, you don't have any rattlesnake meat in that pot, do you?" Sarah peered into the heavy cast-iron kettle hanging over the fire.

"Rattlesnake? Not likely! I let these guys push me just so far. Someone suggested we eat that thing Cliff killed, but I told them they'd have to find another cook."

Sarah chuckled. "Good for you. I bet the women in the 1860s wouldn't have talked back like that."

"Don't you believe it. Remember, most history books were written by men."

Sarah smiled in agreement, but her mind leaped back ten years to a dusty classroom. Another dream—she and Cliff had planned to write the nonsexist history of, well, everything. Dreams had no limits in those days. With a sigh she focused her attention on the task of helping Maureen with the pioneer-style meal.

Despite their difference of opinion over the battle scene, Sarah expected Cliff to join her for breakfast. After all, if they only had today, shouldn't they make the most of it?

To her surprise, he handed her a tin plate, a mug and utensils, then excused himself and went to stand near the fire. Although she caught him following her with his eyes, he remained where he was, sipping coffee from his tin mug and talking with Bill, the tall man in wire-rimmed glasses.

Sarah ate the bacon, biscuit and rice meal silently, trying to pretend Cliff wasn't ignoring her. Was he angry because she'd interrupted his act as a dead soldier or because she'd pushed him earlier?

She restrained herself from seeking him out to apologize and concentrated instead on her meal, which tasted surprisingly good. Sarah doubted if the cavalry in the 1860s had eaten this well, even if the food was basically the same.

"Mind if I join you?" Maureen approached the picnic-table bench, her half-eaten plate of food in one hand and a steaming mug of coffee in the other.

"Not at all." Sarah made room, glad for someone to talk to.

"You looked lonely, and Cliff seems to be engrossed in some discussion with Bill."

"So I've noticed." Sarah pushed the last of her breakfast around her plate. "I hope he's not angry with me about the Indian raid scene. I shouldn't have run into the midst of the battle and spoiled everything, but I didn't realize Cliff was pretending. I thought—"

Maureen patted her arm. "You were only reacting like any other concerned person would react, Sarah. Forget it. Cliff's lucky to have someone around who's worried about him. You two make a cute couple."

"Cliff and I aren't—"

Maureen held up her hand. "I wondered if I'd get a reaction from you with that statement. Just my clumsy way of trying to find out the status of your relationship, which is none of my darn business."

"But there isn't any relationship."

Maureen chuckled. "Of course not. That's why Cliff keeps looking over here with those big cow eyes. And why you raced into the middle of the Indian raid. But that's okay. I said it's none of my business, and I promise to drop the subject." She bit into her bacon and surveyed Sarah with merry green eyes.

Sarah couldn't help the smile that crept across her face, but still she denied Maureen's speculations. "I think you've been watching too many movies, Maureen."

"Probably," said Maureen around another bite of bacon. "But I'll tell you this. Life's too short to waste the kind of thing you seem to feel for each other."

Sarah considered Maureen's statement. She couldn't deny her strong attraction to Cliff. Was it possible for tender emotions to go underground, to flow like a subterranean river undisturbed for ten years, then burst forth, fresh and sparkling, when given an outlet?

"By the way, Sarah," Maureen continued, "did you

want to borrow the brown dress, too? It would look terrific with your coloring. And I won't make a pitch to sell it to you, either."

"Maureen, you're being so nice, and I don't want you to think I wouldn't love to own these dresses, but—"

"It's okay. After all, they are homemade, and—"

"Oh, no! I could never imagine dresses more beautiful than these!"

Maureen studied Sarah for a moment. "I think I'm beginning to understand," she said gently. "His money, his willingness to spend it so freely on you, makes you uncomfortable, doesn't it?"

"Yes," Sarah admitted.

"He only wants to show he cares for you."

"Perhaps, but I—"

"Never mind. Just borrow the brown dress, and we'll be done with it. I have a feeling you and Cliff will work this little problem out eventually." Maureen stood and patted Sarah's shoulder. "I'll get the other dress."

Sarah finished her meal and took her dishes to the hot kettle of dishwater. Cliff was nowhere in sight. She had cleaned the dishes and was looking around for a place to put them when she heard Cliff's strong baritone.

"Thanks, Maureen," he called. "We'll put all this in the tent."

Turning, she saw Cliff approaching her with a pair

of leather high-topped shoes dangling from his hand and the brown dress folded over his arm. Sarah guessed that Maureen had given the clothing to Cliff on purpose to provide him with an excuse to break their awkward silence.

Sarah held up her dishes. "I wasn't sure where to put these."

"If you'll pick up mine—" he nodded toward his own stack "—we'll stow everything away before the next scene is filmed."

Wordlessly Sarah followed his directions and walked with him down the lane between the two rows of tents.

"Just duck under the flap," Cliff directed, holding the canvas back for her to enter. She stooped and preceded him into the warm, musty tent. "Have a seat."

He gestured toward one of two canvas camp stools, and because the tent roof wasn't high enough to allow her to stand, anyway, she sat.

"There." Cliff placed the shoes on his unrolled blanket. "Maureen thinks these will fit." He bent over, hands on his knees, looking from her to the clothing. Suddenly he paled, and with a moan he lowered himself to the tent floor.

Sarah quickly set aside the dishes and dropped to her knees beside him. "Is it your head?"

"Yeah." He closed his eyes. "I guess that leaning-over position isn't so good for me right now."

"Why don't you lie down?" She took hold of his shoulders and started to ease him down on the blanket.

"No! I'll mess up your clothes," he replied, resisting her.

"I'll move them."

"Wait." He caught her wrist, and even as dizzy as she knew him to be, his fingers touched her skin with firm possession. She shivered. "If you'll unroll that other blanket over there, I can lie on that."

Working rapidly, she fashioned the makeshift bed and helped him lie back on the rough wool.

"Sarah, thanks for being here," he said with a sigh. "I feel like such a weakling right now, although earlier my head didn't hurt much at all."

"I guess you were right—it depends on how you move. Remember when you got out of the car and almost fainted?"

"Uh-huh. You were there then, too. You've always been there for me, Sarah. Remember high school? I'd be sweating some campaign speech or worried about the championship football game, and you always came through with a word of encouragement. I...counted on it."

She twisted her hands together. "I'm still playing that role, and unnecessarily, I guess. I'm sorry I ruined the Indian raid scene."

"Don't be. I didn't take your advice, and I put you in a difficult situation when you thought I was hurt. I was afraid if I started a conversation with you at breakfast, you'd use the opportunity to tell me you were leaving so I didn't talk to you at all."

"I thought you were angry."

"Angry because you cared about me? No way." He licked dry lips. "Would you please pour me a drink of water from my canteen? It's a little stuffy in here."

She found the canteen and supported his head and shoulders with one arm while holding the canteen with the other. The solid weight of his broad shoulders was cradled against her, his lips moist and open as he drank. When Sarah lowered the canteen, Cliff's gaze met hers, and she gulped. Heart pounding, she lowered him to the blanket once more, but she couldn't look away from the message in his eyes.

The tent became cozy, too intimate, and a pink flush spread over her freckled skin. She groped for something, anything, to say. "If you're too warm, perhaps you'd like to take off your jacket." Damn, that was the worst comment she could have made!

"Good idea." He began unfastening the brass buttons, and Sarah looked away from the unconsciously provocative gesture.

"And I'll open the tent flap so you can get some more air," she babbled, starting to rise.

"Sarah." Again he grasped her wrist with the same sure grip, as if he were already claiming her. "Don't be afraid of me. After all, I am an injured man."

She didn't feel at all reassured. "I may know that, but I'm not sure you do. Believe me, it would not be good for you to participate in fun and games right now, Cliff. And—and I'm going to see to it that you don't."

He chuckled. "Are you?"

"Yes."

Gently he brought her palm to his lips and placed a kiss there. "Okay, Sarah. If you say so. But this coat is damn hot, and I'd like to relax in here without it. My head hurts, and your cool hand on my forehead feels so great. How about helping me out of this coat and stroking my head for a little while? If you insist, we'll open the tent flaps." He released her hand.

"All right." She moved on hands and knees to the front of the tent and secured the flaps. A cool breeze slipped through the opening, and she sighed, releasing some of the tension curling inside her. She was probably crazy to stay. But he needed her to watch over him during these first hours after his injury. And his father's illness stirred her compassion. At least those were the reasons she gave herself for staying.

Crawling back to his side, she helped him sit up and take off the wool jacket. His white cotton shirt clung damply to his chest. "Let's take the shirt off, too," she said bravely, working at the first wooden button.

"Okay." Cliff shut his eyes and savored the sensation of having her undress him.

"Sit up, please, Cliff."

Her voice was businesslike, but he detected a quiver of her fingers when she slid the material from his body.

"Thanks, Sarah." He settled back on the blanket and looked at her. She avoided his gaze so he closed his eyes again. "Now if you'd stroke my head for a little while..."

He almost moaned aloud at the sweet pleasure of her hand on his forehead. What he would give to be able to bottle that feeling, to have it available for the rough moments of his life. He'd never felt that from a woman's touch. Sarah. His sweet Sarah.

As her fingers stroked his brow, he longed for her hands to explore every inch of his skin. She was magic, and he needed her. How could he keep... His mind drifted to imaginary scenarios in which he and Sarah strolled in slow motion through a hazy watercolor world.

Sarah willed her long fingers to stop their shaking each time she placed her hand on Cliff's forehead. She smoothed back his wavy brown hair and concentrated on controlling her runaway breathing. Taking off his shirt had nearly undone her restored professional attitude. Now he lay half naked in front of her, a fallen hero.

She was aroused by the perfection of his body, made more poignantly beautiful by the injury that sapped his strength. A fallen hero.

Sarah moved her hand across Cliff's brow. She kept her other hand clenched in her lap to keep from caressing his muscled shoulders and arms, his broad chest, the taut skin across his rib cage.

"Sarah?"

"Yes?"

"Got one for you. Who ran against Woodrow Wilson?"

She smiled. "Charles Hughes."

He sighed with satisfaction. "I've missed you, Sarah. Nobody else I know could have answered that."

They were silent for several minutes, and then he spoke again in a dreamy voice.

"You know what we're acting like?"

"No, what?"

"Like two people..." His voice trailed off. Several seconds later he finished the sentence. "Two people falling in...love." His muscles relaxed, and he slept.

4

SARAH GAZED INTO CLIFF'S sleep-softened face. He was right, at least in her case. She was acting like a woman falling in love. She'd been falling for Cliff Hamilton ever since high school. As for him, he was probably confusing love with need. During this difficult time in his life, she offered consolation. He said she'd always been good at that.

So what now? Spend the day with the man she loved, who imagined himself falling in love with her? She could do worse than fulfill her fantasy for one day. A chance to live in Cliff's world, even briefly, wouldn't come again.

She left Cliff's side and sat on the camp stool to put on Maureen's high-topped shoes. While Cliff slept, she'd find out if the movie company would hire another extra. Once outside the tent she ran into Pat and asked whom she should contact.

"Someone should be in that trailer over there." He pointed across the field, then fell into step beside her. "I'll walk you over. How's Cliff?"

"Sleeping. He's not as invincible as he wants everyone to think."

"No kidding. About four years ago he wandered over to our encampment looking like a lost puppy. He'd just been called home from graduate school to help his dad in the business, and he was miserable."

"I'm surprised he didn't join your group."

"No time. Nobody had diagnosed his dad yet, and the old man was screwing up the business faster than Cliff could straighten things out. At least now the poor guy stays at home, out of Cliff's way."

"What a mess. Cliff had such dreams."

"Yeah. He doesn't talk about them much anymore, but he and I got drunk one night, and I found out how important the study of history is to him. He's a scholar, not a businessman."

"You and Maureen are great for including him this weekend, but I hope he doesn't kill himself."

"I'll do my best, but he's hell to keep down. You probably know that."

"In that respect he hasn't changed since high school."

"He seems really happy that you're here, Sarah."

She ignored his remark. "It should be a nice day."

He glanced sideways at her and lifted one dark eyebrow. "Should be. Well, here you are. Tell them I sent you."

"I will. Thanks, Pat."

"No problem. And if Cliff's awake in a half hour or so, Laramour's shooting a cavalry march. Cliff might like to ride in it. I don't think it would bother his head."

Pat tipped his wide-brimmed hat and started back across the field.

Within minutes Sarah was signed with the company for the day's shooting. When the men rode out of camp in the next scene, she would be among the women bidding them goodbye. Despite her misgivings about Cliff, she felt a stir of excitement at the thought of acting in a movie. It would be fun. Her step quickened as she recrossed the field to Cliff's tent.

She peered into the tent opening and found Cliff sitting up, his cotton shirt buttoned but hanging outside his trousers. Seeing her, he stopped brushing the dried blood from his jacket and looked up. Instinctively her hand covered the front of her dress, which gaped open when she stooped to enter the tent.

His glance flickered for a moment, and then he continued brushing his jacket. "Where've you been?"

"Getting hired as an extra. I'm in the next scene and so are you, if you feel up to it." She gathered her skirts under her and sat down across from him.

"I'll be ready. That little catnap really helped."

"Good." Sarah wondered if he remembered his last remark before he'd fallen asleep. Just as well if he didn't. "Does your mother know you're part of the filming this weekend?"

"I mentioned something about it, and I'll check my answering service sometime today. I don't stay out of touch for long."

"Will you tell her about the accident?"

He glanced up. "No. She'll find out when she sees me, and I don't want to give her something else to worry about."

"She's lucky to have you. What would she have done if you hadn't been able to take over the business?"

"Sell it, I guess. I know Dad wouldn't want that, after all his years of work."

"She couldn't learn to run it?"

He looked puzzled. "Mom?"

"Why not? She organized all those charity drives."

"Yeah, but that's different. The real-estate business is dog-eat-dog. She'd never make it."

Sarah opened her mouth to reply, then closed it again. Cliff's opinion of his mother's abilities was not her concern. Still, his flat statement bothered her.

While his attention was focused on his stained jacket, she studied him. The handsome boy of eighteen couldn't hold a candle to the man Cliff had become. His high cheekbones emphasized his deep-set eyes, and the line of his jaw had lost the roundness of youth and now jutted with purpose. Or stubbornness. Why wouldn't he consider his mother as a businesswoman?

Sarah's thoughts were interrupted by the distant sound of a bugle, and she grabbed her purse. "Time to go, and I haven't combed my hair or put on lipstick or..."

"You look terrific. Laramour's liable to sign you to a five-year contract with the studio."

Sarah laughed. "Only if silent films are making a comeback. Remember the time I had to make a speech in front of the student body?"

Cliff groaned. "I'd forgotten. You were pretty terrible. What's your job in this scene, by the way?"

"As the men ride off on the campaign against the Apaches, I'll be one of the camp followers waving goodbye."

"Then I wish we were doing a scene where we're riding back *into* camp. I'd rather be saying hello." He winked at her.

She chose to ignore his insinuation. "If you don't get moving, you won't be in the scene at all."

"You're right." Cliff stood, as much as the height of the tent would allow, and began tucking in his shirt. "It's time for me to get back into my duds, anyway. According to the movies I've seen, a woman can't resist a soldier in uniform, especially if he's on horseback."

"Cliff Hamilton, are you playing soldier to boost your male ego?"

He winked at her. "No, but I'm not above using the image to my advantage."

"I think you'd better get out there, soldier boy, or the parade will go on without you."

"Aye, aye." He scooped up his cap from the floor and swept it toward the tent's open flap. "After you, madam."

Sarah felt his warmth behind her as she scurried from the tent, and before she could move out of reach, he circled her waist with one arm and drew her against him.

"Take care until I get back," he whispered into her ear. His lips nuzzled her neck, and she felt the moist flick of his tongue against her skin.

"Cliff!"

He laughed and released her. "Just getting in character for the movie." He adjusted his cap and gave her a jaunty salute before striding toward the tethered horses.

Sarah followed him with her gaze, but her legs seemed incapable of motion. She was being swept up in the magic of Cliff Hamilton, and she mustn't let that happen! Here, when they playacted nineteenth-century roles, the differences between them appeared insignificant, but what would happen when Cliff returned to his rarefied world and she to her mundane existence?

"There you are, Sarah. I figured you two lovebirds were off somewhere billing and cooing." Maureen smiled. "Are you in this scene, too? Pat said you'd gone to sign up."

"I'm supposed to be one of the camp followers waving goodbye, and if I look worried, I won't be acting." She watched as Cliff swung gracefully up on the big bay gelding. "Cliff makes me nervous riding that tall horse."

"He seems to be a good rider so I wouldn't worry. Come on, Pat's signaling them to fall in." Maureen picked up her skirts as the man with the bullhorn called for the women to gather just outside camp.

"They look just marvelous, don't they, Sarah?" Maureen said, her attention glued to the tall, bearded man heading the mounted column.

"Yes," Sarah answered truthfully, "they do." She remembered Cliff's teasing remarks about women falling for men in uniform, and at this moment she believed it. Cliff sat erect on the big bay, and from her vantage point Sarah couldn't see the white square of gauze taped to the side of his head. With his brass buttons flashing in the sun and his cap tilted casually on his lustrous brown hair, Cliff looked every bit the rakish Union soldier who could break heads or hearts with equal ease.

"You know, Pat's always a better lover when he's captain of F Troop than when he's a grocery-store manager," Maureen confided with a smile. "Something of the excitement of those days transfers to how he feels as a man, and I must admit I feel more like a woman."

As Sarah watched the proud set of Cliff's shoulders, she understood what Maureen was saying. But she would never find out if the same would apply to her. Unconsciously she sighed.

Maureen looked at her sharply. "You're not bored, are you? Some of the extras do get bored."

"Oh, no! Far from it, Maureen."

Maureen gave her a knowing smile. "Good."

"Places, ladies," came the hollow command from

the bullhorn. "The column will ride past you, and you can wave, blow kisses, whatever seems appropriate. You're proud of these guys, and you want to give them a fond farewell before they go off to battle."

Sarah took her place with the others. She could feel the tingle of excitement in the air when the cameras and the klieg lights snapped on. Sabers clanked, saddles creaked and horses snorted as the men filed solemnly past the group of women, who waved and called out their farewells. Sarah could easily imagine the poignancy of such a scene if they really were going to possible death, and she shuddered.

From the corner of her eye, she saw the big bay coming toward her, and she tilted her head back and shielded her eyes from the sun. High atop his horse, with the sun forming a halo around his head and shoulders, Cliff looked magnificent. He was so vibrant, so alive, so real, that suddenly she couldn't imagine her life without him in it.

He flashed her a breathtaking smile. Then, without warning, he swept down and pulled her up to him for a resounding kiss. "No more goodbyes, Sarah," he said, putting her gently back on her feet.

She stood rooted to the spot as the cameras dollied in for a close-up of her dazed expression and her fingers pressed against her mouth as if to suppress a cry of longing.

"Cut!"

The sharp command brought Sarah out of her stupor.

"That was terrific, young lady."

Sarah turned to find a familiar-looking man with a mop of gray hair standing beside her. "Mr. Laramour?"

"At your service."

His perfect smile reminded her of all the years he'd been a matinée idol. She'd been too young to be a fan, but she'd followed his career ever since he'd given up acting and begun making his own movies about the West.

"I'm glad to meet you," she managed, holding out her hand. "I've seen all the Westerns you've directed, and I feel very honored to be involved in this one."

"I knew there was a reason I came over here," he said, laughing. "You're great for my self-confidence. What's your name?"

"Sarah Melton."

"Ever think of taking up acting, Sarah?"

She grimaced. "Hardly. I have no talent."

"I love what you did with that goodbye scene."

"That wasn't acting. That was..." Sarah paused in consternation. Exactly what was the emotion she'd felt as she'd looked up at Cliff?

"Sweetheart, if that wasn't acting, I hope he feels the same way about you."

She looked at him with startled brown eyes. "I can't imagine what you're talking about, Mr. Laramour."

"Oh, I think you can, Sarah Melton. Good luck. And by the way, don't ever cut that gorgeous hair."

Sarah watched him walk back to the camera crew. Martin Laramour was a master at depicting human emotion on the screen. And he had glimpsed the love etched on her face. She'd better be more careful. Beginning now. Pat, Maureen and Cliff were coming in her direction.

"I thought they looked great, didn't you, Sarah?" Maureen said, linking her arm through her husband's.

Sarah nodded. "Very imposing."

"Imposing? Aw, shucks," Cliff said with a grin. "How about devilishly handsome?"

Pat snorted. "If either of you tell him he's devilishly handsome, I'll never hear the end of it. Please don't."

"Then let's talk about how fetching the women looked," Maureen suggested.

"Yeah, let's." Cliff winked at Sarah.

"But I'm dying to see that brown dress on you, Sarah," Maureen continued. "Why don't you wear it next?"

"I'd be glad to, but I need help with all those buttons down the back."

"That's true," Maureen agreed. "Go on over and start changing. I'll come by in a minute to finish up the buttons. If we hurry, we'll make it before they call us for the next scene."

"Why not? Give me five minutes, Maureen." Sarah turned and walked quickly toward Cliff's tent. Once inside she quickly removed the green dress and picked up the brown one. She had it pulled over her head and was fastening the first button at the nape of her neck when Cliff's voice came from outside the tent.

"Sarah? Maureen's been asked to be part of a small scene with Pat. She can't help you right now."

Sarah stopped buttoning. "Okay."

"I can button, too."

"I'm sure you can. Never mind. I'll put the green dress back on." She unfastened the dress and pulled it over her head.

"Don't be silly. I can—"

She whirled around, the brown dress still in her hand, as he ducked under the canvas flap. "Cliff!" She jerked the brown dress in front of her.

"I thought you'd have the thing on by now," he said gruffly.

"I did, but I took it off again. Would you please step outside?"

"Yes, but put the damn thing back on, and let me help you with the buttons. This is ridiculous."

"All right."

When he was back outside, Sarah began to tremble. She tried to tell herself she was embarrassed because Cliff had caught her half dressed. And yet, when he'd come in, covering up wasn't her first instinct. Instead, she'd wanted to move into his arms. Could she sit calmly while he performed the intimate chore of buttoning her dress?

"About ready, Sarah?"

"Yes." She pulled the dress on and buttoned as far as she could reach. "Okay."

When he stepped back into the tent, she avoided his gaze.

"Turn around and sit on the camp stool."

She did as he suggested, and he knelt behind her. He smelled of horses and warm wool, of saddle leather, of another time. Clumsily he worked at the buttons, and his breath on her bare back was shivery delight.

She swallowed hard. "Do you...do you think you'll ever go back to history, Cliff?"

"Doesn't look like it. How about you?"

"I'm going back to school...someday. I'm determined to teach eventually, and write."

"Good. People should do what they love if they possibly can."

"Maybe things will work out for you, Cliff. You never know what—"

"Sarah." He stopped buttoning and rested both hands lightly against her back. "I've become a very practical person. I've accepted what is, not what I'd like to have happen."

"But, Cliff," she began, twisting on the stool to face him. "Without dreams—" As she turned, his arms went naturally around her waist.

"Without dreams I live day to day."

"Sometimes a little recklessly," she guessed. His lips were close, very close.

"Yes. But why shouldn't I take chances? My dad lived carefully all his life and look at him. I intend to get everything I can from life today because who knows about tomorrow?"

Her hands stole up to his shoulders. "I expected more from you, Cliff."

"Maybe I can't live up to your expectations, Sarah." His hands moved along her rib cage and brushed the sides of her breasts. "Maybe I can't be as noble as you'd like."

His touch was heaven. She should make him stop, but the words of protest lodged in her throat.

"I'm just a man, with a man's weaknesses." His eyes darkened. "And at this moment I want you so much I'm going crazy."

"Maureen's right," she murmured, gazing into the caressing blue of his eyes. "There's something about a soldier..."

His eyes smiled into hers. "I was counting on that."

As their lips met, he gathered her against the rough wool of his jacket. She opened her mouth to draw his tongue inside, and she felt his heart pound against her breast as he began undoing the buttons he had so painstakingly fastened.

She shouldn't allow this to happen, she thought dreamily, but his kiss was too sweet, and she wanted just a few moments more in his strong embrace. When he drew the dress down over her arms and let it fall to her waist, she didn't stop him.

His lips moved over her face, bestowing tender kisses. "Let me love you, Sarah. Let me show you how good we can be together." His tongue followed the line of her collarbone, and she leaned away from him, inviting further exploration. "Yes, like that," he murmured, his breath hot on her skin. Deftly he slipped her bra strap over her shoulder and pushed the material down to expose her breast, and she whimpered as his palm nudged the soft flesh up to his waiting mouth.

The warm, moist pressure of his tongue aroused a heat that coursed through her, and her body ached for more. "Oh, Cliff. I want you, too. So much."

His head lifted. "That's all I need to know, Sarah." He smiled at her.

Sarah gazed at him, almost hypnotized, as he half turned to scoop her up and move her to the blanket. Then she noticed his bandage. "Oh, my God." She stiffened in self-reproach. "How could I?"

He settled her on the blanket and glanced sharply at her. "What do you mean?"

"Cliff, this can't happen. You're not well enough! I've been scolding you for being careless with your injury, but what we're heading toward could be just as bad."

"Sarah," Cliff protested, dropping down next to her, "surely, after driving me crazy, you're not going to stop me now." His hand cupped her breast as his eyes swept hungrily over her. "Surely not, Sarah."

She caught his hand and held it against her. "Can

you feel my heartbeat, Cliff? Can't you tell how much I want you, too?"

"Then—"

"No. Not when it might make you worse."

"We could take it slow."

"No." She pulled her strap back in place. "I would never forgive myself if something happened." She saw the agonized look on his face and felt even worse. "Cliff, I'm sorry. I should never have allowed this to go so far, but I—"

"Couldn't help it?" he finished hopefully.

"That's right."

He sighed, then attempted to look more cheerful. "Then I can wait. As long as I know how you feel, we will make love, Sarah. It's just a matter of time."

Sarah looked away. She couldn't tell him that this would be their only day together, that his real life was so different from hers they would have no common ground. Today was a cherished fantasy, but she wouldn't ruin the memory by exposing it to the real world.

5

RELUCTANTLY CLIFF TUGGED her dress up to cover her breasts. "Then we'd better get this on you fast. If I can't love you, it's hell looking at all that kissable skin."

She sat up and pushed her arms into the sleeves. "I'm afraid I still need help with the buttons."

"And somehow I'll find the fortitude to do it. Turn around." Once again he fumbled with the buttons. "Why is it that these are easier to get undone than fastened?"

Sarah chuckled. "Motivation."

"You're right there. Every instinct tells me I'm going in the wrong direction, but I'll try to be patient."

"Cliff, I don't think you should count on anything happening between us. A relationship seems foolish, considering all the—"

"Hey. Let's not analyze anything now. Neither one of us is going to be objective."

She sighed. "I guess you're right."

"Let's concentrate on getting to know each other again. There, all buttoned." He traced the line of her backbone with one finger, and she shivered.

"All right. But go outside while I comb my hair and

get more presentable," she said gently. "I'll only be a minute."

"I'll check on lunch." At the door of the tent, he paused and glanced back. "The brown dress looks terrific, Sarah."

"Thank you."

"Although I prefer it unbuttoned."

"Cliff," she warned.

"Okay. I'm going." He stooped under the tent flap, afterward smoothing it carefully back in place to protect her privacy.

Misgivings assailed her as soon as he was gone. This episode could end up in one wingding of a heartache. Her jeans and shirt, folded and lying in the corner of the tent, caught her eye. She could put them on and be gone before he knew it. Then Sarah laughed out loud. She could never get out of this dress alone. She was trapped.

AS IF TURNING OVER A NEW LEAF, Cliff stayed away from any risky battle scenes for the rest of the day. As the crowd of spectators grew during the filming, Sarah realized how many people hungered for a glimpse of Hollywood in action and also for a glimpse into the past. Cliff served as official tour guide for the camp, and when Sarah wasn't involved in a scene, she answered as many questions as she could from her knowledge of the Civil War period and life on the frontier.

"Aren't those uniforms hot?" a slightly overweight woman with a blond perm asked Cliff.

"Depends on what you do in them," Cliff said and winked at Sarah.

The woman giggled coquettishly. "I see."

"Truthfully, they're a lot cooler than I thought they'd be, but I'd hate to wear this outfit through a Tucson summer."

"You look familiar," the woman observed, eyeing Cliff. "Are you a famous actor?"

"Afraid not. My name's Cliff Hamilton, and I'm from Tucson. I signed on as an extra for the movie."

"Hamilton? Are you Jack Hamilton's son?"

"Yes."

"You and your father have quite a dynasty going up north, don't you?"

Sarah noticed Cliff's expression tighten at the mention of his father.

"I'm not sure you'd call it a dynasty," he hedged. "Lots of other companies—"

"Not like yours! You have that area sewn up, and you're right in the path of big growth, I tell you, big growth." She looked at him curiously. "I heard Jack got sick a couple of years ago. Is he still running the business, or has he left it all to you?"

Picking up her long skirts, Sarah stepped over to Cliff and linked arms with him. "Mr. Hamilton's fine, Mrs...?" She paused for the woman to supply her name.

"Hornquist, Joan Hornquist."

"Well, Mr. Hamilton is just terrific, Joan, and he sends you his love."

"Well, actually, I don't really know him." The woman glanced around nervously.

"Don't you?" Sarah's eyes widened innocently. "From the questions you've been asking, I would have thought you were old friends."

"Not exactly." The woman searched the milling bystanders more frantically. "I'm sure my husband's looking for me," she mumbled. "Nice talking to you, Cliff."

"Nice talking to you, Joan," Sarah called after her rounded form as it disappeared rapidly into the crowd.

Cliff squeezed Sarah's arm against him and grinned down at her. "I've always wondered how to handle people like that. Thanks, Sarah."

"I wouldn't have interfered, but when she started in on your father's health…"

Cliff gazed past her to the craggy mountain range north of the city. "He used to be such a dynamo, Sarah. Could recite real-estate contract clauses by memory. I can't bear for people to know that, these days, he can't remember who I am half the time."

"It must be horrible." She'd seen that sort of agony at the hospital and hated to think it was touching Cliff's life. She wanted to take some of the pain out of those blue eyes. "Don't give up hope. They're discovering something new every day."

The muscles in his jaw tightened. "I won't, and I know he won't. When I think of what he's suffered, my plans to teach history seem pretty selfish, compared to helping him and Mom through this thing."

"No more selfish than me wishing my dad could afford to send me to college when he's always struggled to put bread and butter on the table," she said, thinking only to comfort, forgetting that she hadn't meant to tell Cliff about her family's poverty.

"Is that the only reason you didn't get a history degree? Why, Sarah, that could be so easily fixed. I could—"

"Don't even say it, Cliff," she warned, already berating herself for her outspokenness.

"Sarah, why not? I would love to send you to school. At least one of us could attain the goal we had ten years ago."

"I wouldn't consider it." Sarah removed her arm from his grasp. "You have enough of your own problems, anyway, Cliff."

"Sarah, false pride shouldn't stand in the way of your dreams. Why won't you—"

"Absolutely not!"

"Not another fight, you two." Maureen appeared and took each of them by the arm. "Time to tend the fire for the evening meal, and I need two volunteers to start cooking. Since you seem to have nothing better to do than argue, I choose you."

Sarah allowed herself to be led to the cooking area.

What would she do with this crazy man? Yet she knew what she had to do. She had to explain again that he was rich and she was poor, and the difference made her uncomfortable. As simple as that. Why couldn't he understand?

"We're making a dried-beef-and-rice stew tonight," Maureen explained, picking up a cast-iron pot and handing it to Sarah.

Sarah took the heavy pot. "Rice again? Not much variety in the old days, I guess."

"Not much," Maureen agreed. "Cliff, if you'll put some more wood on the fire, Sarah can fill that pot with water, and we'll get the rice going."

Maureen dispatched them on their tasks as efficiently as a mother dispensing chores to quarreling children. Sarah concluded that perhaps she and Cliff deserved that kind of treatment after the way they'd picked at each other today. Was that what Cliff had meant when he'd said they were acting like two people falling in love?

Maureen chatted steadily throughout the dinner preparations, and as the shadows of the tall cottonwoods lengthened across the campground, the film crew packed up its equipment and left for hotel rooms and restaurant meals, abandoning the park to F Troop for the night.

"It's been fun, but I'm kind of glad they're gone," Maureen confessed as the last of the cameramen drove away. "Now you can see what it's like when we have our encampments minus all the Hollywood touches."

"How often do you do this camping out, 1860s style?" Sarah asked, rapping the spoon against the edge of the cast-iron pot.

"At least three or four times a year with all of us. The men go out more often, but then they get into more serious battle conditions. I'd rather not deal with the snow in the mountains so I'm glad they don't want us along on those weekends."

Cliff shook his head. "The entire idea fascinates me."

"You and Sarah could join, Cliff. I know you're busy, but you need to relax sometime or you'll get ulcers."

"I'll give it serious thought. And I'm sure Sarah would get a kick out of it."

"Cliff, I don't think that I—"

"Don't be hasty, Sarah Jane," Cliff said, tousling her hair. "Looks like we're almost ready to eat, so I'll get a blanket for us to sit on."

Soon he returned with his blanket and spread it on the ground near the crackling logs. As the desert chill crept in from the riverbed, Sarah was glad of the warmth that the cheerful blaze gave off. She noticed with satisfaction that Cliff ate well, which meant his head wound wasn't causing stomach problems. The beef-and-rice stew was amazingly tasty, and Sarah consumed her share.

"Coffee or beer?" Pat asked, coming around the circle with two pitchers.

"Coffee," Sarah said automatically.

"Have a little beer, Sarah," Cliff urged. "Pat orders a special keg for the encampments. I tasted some last night, and it was great."

"Yes, but look at you now," Sarah said, laughing. "Are you *sure* you saw a rattlesnake this morning, or was it a pink elephant?"

"Definitely a rattler," Pat concurred. "Want to see the hide?"

"No, thanks."

"Then how about some beer?" he asked, lifting his eyebrows challengingly.

"Fine." Sarah stuck out her tin cup. She might as well play this pioneer life to the hilt.

"I'll have a little beer, too, Pat," Cliff said, holding out his cup. He glanced sideways at Sarah. "That is, if my nurse thinks I can."

"A small cup won't hurt, I guess. You seem to be fine."

Cliff's reference to Sarah's nursing duties reminded her that the day was officially over. Soon she must leave but not just yet. The fire was warm, and the beer was very good.

"Here's to us," Cliff whispered, raising his mug in Sarah's direction.

"Here's to your health," Sarah whispered back, taking a sip.

"I'll drink to that." He watched the firelight burnish Sarah's hair to a coppery sheen, and he longed to run his fingers through it. Someday, by God, he'd make love to her.

Sarah was very aware of Cliff's body next to hers on the blanket. She could hear him breathing, smell the subtle aroma of woodsmoke and warm wool that clung to him. She drained her mug. "This beer is very good."

"You're flushed," Cliff said softly, stroking her cheek. "Too much beer or too much heat from the fire or—" he looked at her speculatively "—I wonder, Sarah Jane. Could my prim and proper longtime friend be thinking the same thing I am?"

"I doubt it," she lied, gazing into the flames. A log burned through and fell into the embers, sending sparks swarming upward like disturbed honeybees. Sarah watched the sparks gradually cease their furious climb until at last they moved upward in lazy spirals, winking out one by one. Her eyelids drooped. From the other side of the circle came the strumming of a guitar, and a sweet lassitude settled over her.

"Come here, Sarah." Gently Cliff slid his arm around her waist, and she leaned gratefully against his shoulder.

"Poor Sarah," he crooned against her forehead. "I didn't stop to think that you'd been up all night when we left the hospital. You must be exhausted."

"No, no," she protested sleepily, covering a yawn with her long fingers. "I'll rest for a little while and have some coffee." She settled more comfortably into the curve of his shoulder, and her lashes fluttered to her cheeks. "Don't let me go to sleep," she mumbled.

He murmured something noncommittal and pulled her closer, relishing the feel of her in his arms again. How beautifully her body curved into his, and he didn't have to stretch his imagination much to know what she'd feel like under him. He'd fit into her like a sword into its sheath.

After that morning he had decided she'd had at least one lover in her life. She knew something of the responses between a man and a woman. After all, she was twenty-five years old. But he'd bet money on her old-fashioned values. She may have had sex with someone, but she hadn't given the guy everything, not that deep center core. Once she did, there would never be another man for her. The thought unsettled him.

"You've grown into quite a woman, Marvelous Melton," he said into her smoke-scented hair.

"Mmm." She stirred drowsily, and he bent to press his lips against her cheek.

"I don't think you'll be able to kiss your sleepyhead awake, Cliff," Pat said, coming around the circle for refills of coffee and beer. "She looks like she's out for the duration. Why not let her lie down in your tent and come back and join us for a while?"

"Good idea, Pat. But I think I'll turn in, too."

Pat held his friend's steady gaze. "Okay."

"Don't worry. I won't take advantage of a groggy woman."

"I never said you would. Need any help carrying her in?" Pat paused in the act of pouring Maureen more beer.

"I can manage."

"She's a sweet girl."

"Yes, Pat. I'll remember that." Carefully he shook Sarah almost awake, then drew her gently up to lean against him. He knew she wasn't fully conscious, but that was better. She wouldn't realize exactly what was happening until they were safely in the tent. He had said she could back out anytime, but time had run out.

Maureen hurried over and tucked a soft bundle under his arm. "Give her this to put on so she won't wrinkle her dress."

"Thanks, Maureen," he whispered.

"Thanks, Maureen," Sarah murmured dreamily as they left the warm circle of the fire. "One beer doesn't usually do this to me," she added.

Cliff pulled her closer. "It's not the beer, Sarah. You're tired. You need to sleep."

"Can't sleep. Got to keep an eye on you," she said. She stumbled once, and he caught her more firmly to him.

He smiled to himself. Did she want to keep an eye on him because of his safety, or hers? "I'll be fine," he said reassuringly.

She relaxed against him, then stooped obligingly as he helped her through the door of the tent. When the flap fell closed behind them, he felt like shouting for joy. Alone with his Sarah.

Carefully he placed her on the blanket and lit the kerosene lamp standing ready in a corner of the tent. He could do this in the dark, but why should he? Kneeling beside her, he turned her on her side and began unbuttoning her dress. Her eyes fluttered open. "Cliff? I can do the rest after you finish with the buttons," she murmured, but her eyes closed again, and her hands were still.

"I know." He finished with the buttons and unfastened the back clasp of her bra. Then he rolled her back and pulled the garments from her body. For long moments he sat and savored the gentle rise and fall of her uncovered breasts. Last summer's tan lingered, announcing with its golden border that she had braved the Arizona sun in a bikini.

A fist of desire formed in his gut as he reached involuntarily for the ivory newness of the skin the sun hadn't touched, but he drew back. Better not start that, if he expected to keep himself in check.

A breeze ruffled through the tent flaps, and her nipples tightened in response to the chill. God, how he wanted to touch her! More roughly than he'd intended, he lifted her hips to pull the dress away, and she moaned softly in her sleep. "Sorry, sweetheart," he apologized as he worked the gown past her legs and feet.

She murmured something he couldn't understand

and rolled to her side. Her arms closed over her breasts, and she curled her knees up protectively. The childlike position helped him get a rein on his runaway passion, and he stroked her hair back from her face. "You don't have to close into a little ball because of me, Sarah," he crooned. "Very soon you'll realize that you can drop your guard. I won't hurt you."

Rapidly he completed his task. When he slid the smooth nylon panties over her hips, he deliberately made his mind blank. To allow himself to think of the soft blond triangle he uncovered would unleash all his animal instincts, and her female scent made them clamor to be loosed.

Grabbing the long-sleeved flannel nightgown Maureen had provided, he popped it over her head and soon had it pulled down to her ankles. "Shoes. I forgot to take off your shoes," he murmured and forced his shaking fingers to unlace the confining leather. "Sarah, you'll never know what a mixture of pleasure and pain this undressing process was," he said with a sigh as he pulled a blanket over her sleeping form.

He shrugged out of his jacket and sat on his bedroll to pull off his own boots, socks and wool trousers. Clad only in his shirt and underwear, he extinguished the kerosene lamp and lay on his rough blanket listening to her breathe.

He couldn't remember ever being so conscious of another human being, yet her presence seemed to fit the natural order of things, as if he'd always known

Sarah would someday sleep peacefully at his side. Funny, but he'd never imagined marriage to anyone until now. Marriage. Now that was a sobering thought.

The painful twinges from his stitches had nearly stopped. The healing process was under way, and he knew instinctively that he would suffer no complications from his accident. Closing his eyes, he set his mental alarm for five in the morning.

HOURS LATER, Sarah stirred uncomfortably. Beer always did this to her, and now she'd have to leave this warm bed and stumble to— She sat up abruptly. Good God, she was in Cliff's tent, had been all night. A vague memory returned—of Cliff helping her walk, a chill when he changed her clothes. Changed her clothes!

She touched the sleeve of her nightgown. Sure enough, Cliff had put her in this getup. Probably from Maureen's cache. Sarah's cheeks burned at the thought of everyone knowing she was sleeping in Cliff's tent. She moaned softly and glanced around her. The inside of the tent was very dark, and Cliff was only a lumpy shadow on the other side.

She sighed in resignation. First things first. Wrapping the warm blanket around her, she scuttled barefoot into the cold night, found the park rest rooms and took care of her most urgent problem. By the time she slipped back into the tent, her teeth were chattering.

What time was it? Should she leave now before anyone woke up? She found her pocket watch and held it very close to her face. Looked like four-thirty. She inched gingerly toward Cliff, trying to make sure he was sound asleep so that she could dress and get away.

"Sarah?"

Damn. "What?"

"Are you all right?"

"I'm f-fine. Go b-back to sleep, Cliff."

"You sound cold." He reached for her and captured her wrist. "Your arm is freezing. Come here, and I'll warm you up."

"That's okay." Could he feel her pulse racing? "I'll go back to my own bed. These wool blankets are quite warm, and in no time I'll be—"

"Sarah."

"What?"

"Stop playing games with me."

"I'm not."

"Your arm is warmer already. Let me do a complete job."

"Cliff, go back to sleep." She tried to pull her wrist from his firm grasp. "You need your rest."

"I need something else a lot more, Marvelous Melton."

6

SARAH COULDN'T PRETEND IGNORANCE of his meaning. But making love to this man would be far too dangerous. She fumbled for the first excuse she could think of. "Cliff, no. Your head."

"My head feels fine."

She stalled. "How long have you been awake?"

"Since you have." He stroked the inside of her wrist with his thumb. "When you sat bolt upright, I knew you were disoriented so I didn't want to speak out loud and scare you. I was a little concerned when you left the tent."

"The, uh, beer. I, ah..."

"I figured that out."

"Why did you let me crawl over here without saying a word?"

"You think I'm going to risk messing up a good thing? How did I know why you were scooting to my side of the tent?"

"It wasn't what you think."

"Wasn't it?"

"No, I..." But she wondered. Had she wanted him to

wake up and stop her from running away? Her heart began to pound.

"Sarah, I want you," he said softly. "Yesterday you wanted me, too."

Yes, she had. Gently he pushed back her sleeve and stroked the fine hair on her arm. She trembled in response. She swallowed hard, then forced an answer from her unwilling throat. "I don't think it's wise."

His fingertips found the inside of her elbow and made lazy circles. "Are you always wise, Sarah Jane?"

She smiled tremulously. "Of course. I'm the eldest child, wise beyond her years."

Cliff strained to see her expression, but the darkness hid her reaction to him. He didn't want to blunder because he was misreading her feelings.

Propping himself on one arm, he moved his other hand up over her shoulder to the nape of her neck. The moist tendrils of her hair flowed through his spread fingers as he urged her closer. He could feel the warmth of her breath on his face.

"Sometimes," he murmured, "it's wise to be foolish."

Sarah was powerless to stop the kiss, even knowing what must inevitably follow. In unhurried fashion, as if he knew she wouldn't turn aside, Cliff closed the gap until their breath mingled.

His deliberate mastery of her mouth left no doubt as to how he expected this interlude to end, and as she opened to his questing tongue, she realized there could be no turning back this time. When his hand moved from her neck to circle her waist and pull her down next to him, she didn't resist.

He fit her tightly against him, groaning softly at the ripe promise of her so close, only scant bits of material separating them. He unfastened the button at the high neck of her gown. "Lift your arms," he whispered against her mouth.

Reaching for the nightgown's hem, he skimmed the garment over her head. Then he unbuttoned his shirt and gathered her into his arms, pressing the fullness of her soft breasts against his hair-roughened chest. "God, you feel fantastic," he said with a sigh as his lips covered hers.

She arched against him, molding her hips to the pulsing desire covered by his cotton briefs. The darkness surrounded them in a hushed cave of intimacy, urging Sarah to abandon reason, to surrender herself to this delirious passion.

Cliff's mouth left hers and found the hard bud of one nipple. The tug of his teeth and lips made her writhe against him, and her breathing grew ragged.

"Love me," she begged, almost afraid the moment would slip away. She tugged at his briefs, and he lifted his hips so she could remove the last bit of clothing between them. "Love me now."

He gasped as her warm fingers encircled him. "Not yet, Sarah," he said, his voice coarsened with desire. "I want to see you. I'm going to light the lamp."

"No," she murmured, suddenly aware of where they were. "Light casts shadows."

"The others are asleep. I want to watch your face while I love you." His lips lingered against hers for a moment, then were gone.

He left a cold void, a place where doubts and misgivings crept in and lay beside her. She closed her eyes and tried to regain the security of a moment ago.

Her eyelids flew open at the tiny scratch announcing Cliff had found the matches. As the flame flickered in his cupped hands, the small blaze illuminated his face, creating fierce shadows. Sarah trembled, both from anticipation and fear that she was making a terrible mistake.

He lifted the lantern's chimney with a practiced hand and ignited the kerosene-soaked wick. Light leaped into every corner of the tent, and Sarah instinctively turned away from the sudden brightness and the uncompromising view of his desire for her. The glare softened as he turned down the wick.

"Don't be shy, Sarah." Cliff pulled her slowly over to face him on the rough blanket. "Am I so difficult to look at?"

She winced at the vulnerability in his voice. "Of course not. You're...extremely...very... I'm just not used to this, I guess. You were my high school idol, and now..."

"Now I'm just a man who wants you very much."

He cupped her chin and looked deep into her eyes. "I hope you want me, too."

Her heart raced in response to the heat of his gaze. No matter what the consequences, she had to have him. "Yes, I want you."

"Thank God. You're so beautiful, Sarah." His hand followed the curve of her neck to the slope of one breast, and he teased the tip to rigidity with his thumb. Watching the play of emotions on her face, he moved to caress her other breast. "That's what I wanted. To see that look in your eyes. And to enjoy all of you."

His thirsty gaze traveled over her, delighting in the heavy fullness resting in his palm. He bent to kiss the tiny freckle over her heart, the valley between her breasts. When she sucked in her breath, he followed the line of her ribs and dipped his tongue into the hollow of her navel.

"Cliff," she moaned.

"Yes, I'm here."

His touch made her shiver then burn as he caressed her lightly and soon with firm intent, until she was whimpering softly.

"So beautiful, Sarah," he murmured.

"I want you," she said breathlessly. "I want you inside me, Cliff."

She reached for him, and he trembled at her touch. "I know. But I meant to—"

"Love me, Cliff," she whispered, and her fingers closed urgently around him.

With a moan of assent, he moved over her. As he thrust forward, she rose to meet him, giving herself as he hadn't dared to expect she would. With a hushed cry he sought the moist, velvet depths of her, and she answered with a gasp of delight at the fusion of their bodies.

"Sarah," he said raggedly as she closed herself around him and he felt wondrously lost in her. "At last, Sarah."

"Yes, Cliff," she crooned. The ageless rhythm of his movements was transforming her, taking away the empty ache and replacing it with blossoming fulfillment. The sharp excitement Cliff had given her before was nothing compared to the total involvement she felt now, and her heartbeat became a crescendo of drums as Cliff took her further and further into herself.

Ever deeper he plunged, discovering new levels of abandon in her. And when he thought she could open herself no more, she flung back the inner gates to her passionate soul, allowing him to touch the core of her being; she seemed to cascade over him like a shimmering waterfall. With a soft cry of triumph, he followed her into his own shattering release.

For long moments they lay entwined, not speaking, savoring the gifts they had bestowed upon each other. Then Sarah opened her eyes slowly and stared at the golden light the lamp cast on the tent roof. She felt filled with the same kind of butterscotch happiness.

"Sarah Jane, for someone who doesn't live recklessly, you make love with the daring of a sky diver," Cliff said into her ear. "I have never known a woman who threw herself into the experience like that."

"Cliff—" her voice was tinged with awe "—I've never behaved that way before."

He raised himself on one elbow to look at her. "You haven't?"

"No, I—" She stopped in confusion. "That was dumb to admit, wasn't it?"

"Why?"

"Now you're liable to feel some obligation to me. I don't want that."

"What if I told you I've never experienced anything like that with a woman? Would you be obligated to me?"

She stared at him. "This is getting out of hand. I never intended—"

"What did you intend? I don't picture you as a one-night stand person, Sarah. And I'm sure as hell not."

"No, no, that's not what I wanted, either. But we can't—this isn't the beginning of— Damn, why didn't I leave last night?"

"You regret what just happened."

"Yes. No. I don't know." She looked away from the anxiety on his face. "We're so different, Cliff. This time together has been special, but it's not the real world. Continuing this relationship would be unwise—for both of us."

"Ah. Unwise again. What's the problem? A very

large boyfriend? An unspeakable hereditary trait in your family?"

"Much worse than that. It has to do with the kind of people we are—where we've been and where we're going." How she wanted to hold back the words, but she was afraid the hurt would get worse with every passing moment. "Please don't plan on anything more than we've shared this weekend."

She kept her face averted, not wanting to see the pain and disappointment her statement would inflict. If only this could have been said later. If she hadn't opened her mouth about her reaction to their lovemaking, they might have enjoyed each other's company until the encampment broke up this afternoon. She would have disappeared from his life and he from hers.

Almost roughly he brought her back to face him. "Sarah Jane, you're not making a hell of a lot of sense. And I'm planning on quite a bit more than we've shared this weekend. I've rediscovered my lost Sarah, and I have ten years of catching up to do."

"It's too late, Cliff."

"Never." He nibbled her lower lip. "In fact, not even slightly too late. I'd say we found each other in the nick of time." He gave her a quick squeeze and released her, then reached out to extinguish the kerosene lamp.

Pale sunshine crept under the tent flap. "Obviously we need to have a long talk about this," Cliff continued, "but it's getting light, and I have to feed the horses. That's the deal I insisted on with Pat in return for eating his food."

"I've been eating his food, too. I should—" She bit back the rest of the sentence. Instinctively she wanted to go with him, but if he left alone, she'd have the opportunity to do what must be done.

"Help? It's sweet of you to offer, but why don't you stay here and rest?" Gently he untangled his legs from hers. "I'll be back soon, especially if I don't meet any snakes this time around."

He hadn't heard what she'd been saying. Not really. She forced herself to smile up at him. "Be careful, okay?"

"You bet. I have a reason to be, now."

Even in the dim light she could see the purpose in his blue eyes. Long ago she had thrilled to that look, believing Cliff Hamilton could accomplish anything. But this time the cards were stacked against him. Against them both...

With economy he pulled on his clothes, and she closed her eyes so he wouldn't see her tears.

"And when I get back, we'll discuss this terrible incompatibility you imagine we have."

She murmured something vague and drew the blanket over her shoulders. She had made her decision. After he left, she would dress in her jeans and shirt and leave before he missed her. Better to end the fantasy now before the differences in their lives eroded the closeness they had found in these few hours.

Cliff buttoned his jacket and crouched beside her. "Keep the home fires burning while I'm gone, lovely camp follower," he whispered, kissing her cheek.

Sarah swallowed and opened her eyes, but his image blurred, and she squeezed her lids shut again.

"Don't cry, Marvelous Melton. I have a hunch you're making a mountain out of several small molehills." He smoothed her copper hair away from her face. "We'll work it out, Sarah. Just relax now, and don't put that brown dress on until I get back, okay? I'm going to bring some hot water and give you the most wonderful sponge bath you've ever had."

"That sounds nice," she said wistfully.

"It will be," he promised, then kissed her hard on the lips. "I'll be back."

She watched him disappear from the tent, and her throat knotted with grief. But she had to go. Better that their memories of each other remain untarnished.

The interior of the tent twisted out of focus as tears gathered in her eyes, yet she scrambled determinedly from the rude bed and found her pile of clothes. After the smooth drape of Maureen's dresses, the denim felt rough on her bare legs, and the short-sleeved pullover lacked any feminine grace.

What difference did that make? The rasp of the zipper underscored her misery. She'd been playing make-believe, and the game was over. Time to get back to the real world.

She tied her athletic shoes with a vengeance, nearly

cutting off the circulation to her foot, but slowed her movements while folding Maureen's beautiful clothes. Dresses like these couldn't be handled with the dispatch of jeans and T-shirts.

After placing the dresses in a neat pile, she located her purse and started for the door. She turned back one last time to fix the scene firmly in her mind, to remember clearly what this tent looked like, how she had felt learning the wonder of love with Cliff. Leaving now seemed so cold, but there was no other way.

"What in the hell are you doing?"

She whirled and bumped into him, sending warm soapy water from the basin he carried sloshing over both of them.

"Cliff! I'm sorry. I—"

He put the dripping basin on the tent floor, then stood up as far as the tent ceiling allowed and looked at her. His eyes narrowed. "You were going to leave. Just like that. Without saying anything to anyone."

"It's better if I go."

"Who's it better for?"

"Both of us."

"The hell it is. Leaving is the cowardly way out, Sarah. Stay and prove you're not a coward."

"But I am." Her dark eyes pleaded with him for understanding. "I don't want to spoil what we had with harsh realities, Cliff. Let me have my dream."

"Stay, and I'll make more dreams come true."

"No. I won't take the chance. I'm leaving, Cliff."

"What about the filming? You obviously don't give a damn about me, but you signed on as an extra, remember?"

"I doubt if I'll be missed much."

"What happened to dependable Sarah?" he said desperately, grasping at any tactic to hold her there.

"She made a mistake early this morning. Remaining here any longer would be another bigger one."

"Maureen and Pat will be hurt, Sarah."

"I know. Would you tell them how much I appreciate all they did for me?"

He stared at her without answering. "What about the money you earned?"

Her eyes were bleak. "I can't afford to stay and collect it. Goodbye, Cliff." With a sob she pushed through the tent flap and ran out into the pale light of morning.

He could have grabbed her, forced her to listen to him, but he didn't, sensing the futility of forcing Sarah Jane Melton to do anything. He stepped out of the tent and fought the urge to run after her as she raced toward her fire-engine-red Volkswagen.

"Hey, Cliff, thanks for feeding the horses and putting the coffee on." Pat strode forward, a steaming cup in one large hand.

"No problem."

"Is that Sarah getting into that red car?"

"Yes."

"She's not leaving?"

"Afraid so." Cliff cleared his throat. "She asked me to thank both you and Maureen for your kindness."

"She's not coming back later?"

"No."

Pat glanced uneasily at his friend. "I gather something major happened between you two."

Cliff's gaze moved past Pat to the sunlit flanks of the mountain range. "You might say that," he said at last.

"Gonna do anything about it?"

Cliff laughed bitterly. "Sure. I'm going to leave my mother in the lurch with the business, donate my house and car to charity and become a poor history professor."

"Sarah wants you to do that?"

"Of course not. But she insists on making my money and life-style an insurmountable problem between us. How can I battle that kind of thinking?"

Pat sipped his coffee. "Convince her she's wrong."

"I know that woman. She's not easily convinced of being wrong."

"Is it worth trying?"

Cliff looked at his friend and sighed. "Yep."

7

As soon as she walked in the door of her tiny apartment, Sarah reached for the goldfish food.

"Poor Mabel and Manfred." She sprinkled the dry flakes across the calm surface and watched guiltily as the fish rocketed upward to gobble the food. "About to starve because your mistress was out cavorting with a man." Her lips trembled on the last word, and before she could control her tears, they coursed down her cheeks and fell with a light patter into the fishbowl.

"You g-guys don't know how easy you've got it," she stammered as the tears flowed faster. "Safe in your little world. You'll never m-meet anyone but each other."

Mabel and Manfred skimmed the top of the water, their puckered mouths clearing the surface of any floating food. Then they plummeted in unison to root through the gravel for any remaining morsels.

"I should have gotten a dog," Sarah muttered. "You can put your arms around a dog when you need comfort. What comfort are a couple of hungry fish?"

But she knew why she didn't have a dog. Dogs ate a lot, and had to have shots, and a collar and leash, and a yard. "Damn it, why does there have to be such a thing as money? Money fouls everything up!" She threw her purse on the couch and stomped into the bathroom.

Angrily she pulled off her clothes and threw them into the wicker hamper she'd bargained hard for in Mexico. "Why have I had to struggle for everything? *Everything*?" she wailed as she twisted the hot-water handle. The water drizzled out, and with a groan of frustration she turned the handle again. "Of course there's no water pressure. Of course not."

While waiting for the water to heat, she surveyed the tiny bathroom. Like the entire apartment, it was painted a utilitarian off-white. To counter the stark effect, Sarah used bright red in every decorating touch—towels, kitchen tablecloth, throw pillows, curtain ties and her flowered bedspread all contained at least a splash of red.

Usually the color cheered her but not this morning. This morning the bathroom seemed small, the apartment depressing, her life incredibly dull. What was Cliff doing right now?

"I don't care!" she shouted into the spray. "I am going to forget about him!"

Three loud thumps sounded on the wall opposite her. "Sorry, Ethel!" she called through the wall. "I forgot it was Sunday."

She and Ethel had come to an understanding a year ago when they'd realized the wall dividing their duplex allowed every sound to pass through. Ethel went

to her cafeteria job early every morning except Sunday.
But on Sunday the sixty-two-year-old woman slept in,
and Sarah walked on tiptoe until noon.

"I bet Cliff has acres and acres to shout in," she muttered, turning off the shower. "Well, at least I have one.
There's no house on it yet, but someday I'll have a
house on my acre. Someday."

Thinking of the land she hoped would be her share
of her great-grandfather's undeveloped homestead,
Sarah realized that she hadn't visited her family in two
weeks. Today was as good a day as any, and it might
keep her mind off Cliff for a few hours.

The drive to Catalina soothed her jangled nerves.
She loved this part of the old Florence Highway as it
curved around the tail end of the Santa Catalinas and
afforded a view of the back side of the mountain range.
Civilization had only made tentative inroads here compared to the multiplying foothills developments on the
Tucson side of the range. The back side was a little
cooler, a little greener, a little wilder.

She considered turning off the highway to spend
some time at her great-grandfather's homestead. The
adobe house had crumbled years ago, and gradually
the land had lost all imprint of a man's hand except for
the narrow dirt road leading onto the property.

For years Sarah had used the homestead as a refuge
whenever she had to wrestle with a problem, but she
could wrestle all day and not find a solution to the
problem of Cliff. She had to forget him. For that she

needed the company of people who loved her, not solitude.

As she drove on toward Catalina, Sarah thought of her mother and father and their unrealized dreams. Ever since she could remember, they had talked about drilling a well on those ten acres, putting in electricity, building a house. Extra money had never been available.

Extra money. Sarah wondered if her parents had ever known what spare change felt like jingling in your pockets. Probably not. She sighed and made the familiar turn down the lane leading into her parents' property. Within minutes she pulled up next to her father's dusty pickup.

"Sarah!" Her youngest brother leaped from the porch of the double-wide mobile home and ran to greet her. "I got three Excellents on my report card last time, Sarah!" He caught her hand in his grubby one. "And you haven't seen the barnyard I'm building in my room for those little animals you gave me, and Mittens is going to have babies again, and Dad says one more batch of kittens is too many, but I can—"

"Slow down, sport," Sarah coaxed, feeling better already. "I'll be here all day, so you don't have to cram every bit of news into the first five seconds."

"All day? Far out! Watch my new batting stance." He crouched down, his hands grasping an imaginary bat.

"Looks good, slugger."

"Mom and Dad said I *might* be able to go out for Little League this year if..."

Sarah knew by heart the end of the sentence Eddie didn't finish. If we can afford it. Little League was cheap but not free. And players needed a glove, and most of them wore cleats. She'd like to treat Eddie to the whole expense, but her mother and father wouldn't consider letting her do it. Maybe if she found a used glove for sale, she could convince them that a friend gave it to her. Only then could she present such a valuable gift to Eddie.

"I hope you'll be able to play, Eddie," she said, squeezing his shoulder. "Where is everybody? Think I could get some lunch around here?"

"Mom's fixing bologna sandwiches right this minute. Come on." Eddie tugged her up the porch steps and into the mobile home.

THE AFTERNOON SPED BY, and more than once Sarah inwardly thanked her boisterous family for taking her mind off Cliff. When they begged her to stay for supper, she agreed. She didn't have to work until eleven Monday night, and she didn't want any more empty hours to fill than necessary.

After the meal Sarah picked up a dish towel and began drying dishes for her mother. "Eddie mentioned you might let him sign up for Little League this year."

Her mother gazed out the kitchen window at the fading light. "You know how it is with eight-year-old boys in the spring. So many of his friends will be in it, but I'm not sure we can come up with the wherewithal. It's not just the twenty-dollar registration fee but the mitt, and he thinks he needs cleats, and—"

"No word that the mine will be calling back more people?"

Ann Melton turned, and Sarah noticed that the lines traced by years of worry had become more pronounced in her mother's face. She realized with a shock that her mother was aging.

"The copper industry will never be what it once was, Sarah," she said in a low voice. "You know that." She glanced toward the living room and satisfied herself that the volume of the television set would mask their conversation from the rest of the family. "Your father has talked about retraining for another job many times."

"That would cost money, too." But Sarah wondered if money would be the only obstacle. Her father was fifty-four years old, and mining had been his whole life. Could he begin all over again?

"There...there is a way, and I guess we'll have to take it." Sarah's mother scrubbed at the pot in her hand, as if getting it clean would solve all her problems. "We can sell some of Grandpa's land."

"No!" The word was out before Sarah could stop herself.

Sarah's mother scrubbed harder at the bottom of the pot, and when she spoke, her tone was defensive. "I don't like it, either, but we're talking about survival. We can't afford to develop that land. Perhaps we never will be able to so we might as well turn some of it into cash. It's worth quite a bit now, at least ten thousand an acre."

"How can you talk like that, as if it's just a—a commodity? That land is our heritage!"

"Hush, Sarah. Your father will hear."

"You haven't told him?"

"Of course I have. We've discussed it in detail. I promised him none of us would be upset." She gave Sarah a significant look.

"Too bad, Mom. I'm upset."

"Sarah—"

"All my life I've dreamed of the day when you'd sign over a part of that land to me for my house."

"We won't sell it all. Maybe just two acres on the south side."

"That's my favorite spot!"

"Al Hollencraft advised us that would be the easiest section to sell because it's closest to Tucson."

"You and Dad have already called the real-estate man?"

"Yes." Her mother washed dishes furiously.

"This is ridiculous. I have a fair amount saved. Not twenty thousand dollars, but several thousand. Let me help instead of selling the land."

"No. That's your college fund."

"The land is more important to me than college. I'll go to school later."

Her mother turned and grasped her shoulders with soapy hands. "No, Sarah. You've become falsely sentimental about some stupid piece of ground. Use your money for college. It's your ticket to a better life."

"Don't sell the land, Mom."

"We have to, Sarah. Not just for your dad's school, but for debts, for the boys' clothes, dentist bills, even Eddie's Little League. Try to understand."

Reluctantly Sarah acknowledged the desperation in her mother's eyes. "Mom, I'm sorry." She took a deep breath and put her arms around her mother. "This family's more important than some old piece of land." The words almost wouldn't come out, but she had to say them.

Images crowded her mind—of special private hours spent walking "her" acre, counting "her" paloverde trees, gazing up at "her" saguaro. The giant cactus was the largest of the entire thirty-acre parcel and at last count boasted twenty arms. Quite possibly it was more than two hundred years old, and Sarah loved to stand next to it and feel as if she were reaching back in time.

"I'm the one who's sorry, Sarah." Her mother stood still within Sarah's embrace. "You never have gotten what you wanted out of life, have you?"

Sarah gave her mother a squeeze. "I've gotten my share, Mom. I've got you. I've got Dad. I've got five little brothers, all smart as whips. I'm healthy, and I have a job. That's a lot."

"These days it is."

Sarah hugged her once, hard, then released her, afraid they both might be in tears if she prolonged the contact. "It'll work out. What does Dad want to do?"

"Would you believe he's talking about computers?"

"Why not? It's the wave of the future, isn't it?"

Her mother smiled, and this time a little of the sparkle Sarah remembered was in her eyes. "I swear that man amazes me." She lifted her arms to remove two of the bobby pins from the thick coil of brown hair atop her head. "Been working hard labor in a mine all his life," she continued, jabbing the pins more firmly into her shiny hair, "and now he plans to turn everything around and sit at a desk."

"Could he stand that?"

"I don't know. Never thought I'd see the day when he went to work in a shirt and tie, but he sounds determined."

Sarah felt a surge of pride in her father. Inevitably she thought of Jack Hamilton and Cliff's agony over his father's deterioration. She had a lot to be thankful for. "You'd better put that property on the market, Mom."

"Al's coming out this week."

"Good idea." This week. Sarah tried to hide her dismay. Soon her land would be gone.

"If we don't get any action from someone local, we

may go to one of the bigger companies in Tucson," her mother added.

Sarah's breath caught at a new possibility. Hamilton Realty would be the obvious choice. "I'm sure you'll do fine with this first one," Sarah babbled, as much to reassure herself as her mother. "He knows the territory."

"We'll see. In the meantime, your dad is starting the training, and the school's agreed to defer the tuition payments until we sell the land."

Sarah lifted an eyebrow. "When you began this conversation, you said Dad was *thinking* of retraining. Now you say he's already enrolled. You were holding out on me."

"Your dad didn't want me to say anything yet, and he hated to tell you about the land. So did I."

"And I acted like a spoiled brat. Forgive me." Sarah smiled warmly, determined that her mother would not suspect how deeply the loss of the land affected her. She touched the gold watch in her jeans pocket. At least she still had that.

"Somebody named Hamilton was in looking for you a couple of mornings ago, Sarah."

She glanced up, startled, at the orderly.

"You'd already left so he said he'd try again." The orderly smiled and walked down the hall.

Sarah swallowed and looked at the clock. A half hour to go. But maybe Cliff wouldn't try again. Maybe he only said so to be polite. But what if he showed up today? The car accident victims she had X-rayed had left the front of her smock spattered with blood. She hadn't had time to change.

At five minutes to seven, as she was filing the last set of X rays, he walked in. His smile faded when she turned away from the filing cabinet.

"My God, Sarah."

"Hello, Cliff."

"Your clothes are covered with blood."

"Busy morning. Bad car accident." She concentrated on taking slow, even breaths. "How are you?"

"I don't like to think of you exposed to—"

"The real world?" she snapped.

"That's not what I meant. But, Sarah, all that blood."

"Sorry, but that's how I make my living. I warned you about reality and how it might affect our relationship. Now you can see for yourself."

"Stop it, Sarah. Despite what you think, I'm not some sheltered rich kid. I brought my father in for some tests this morning, and if that's not reality, I don't know what is."

Remorse shadowed her brown eyes. She shouldn't have reacted so sharply before finding out exactly why he was here. "I'm sorry, Cliff. Is your father worse?"

"I think so. It's hard for me to tell."

Sarah laid her hand on his arm, wanting to comfort him. "I'll be through in five minutes. Can I see him?"

Cliff's hand covered hers, and his warmth felt good— very good.

"Thanks for offering, but he's not the same man, Sarah. It might be better if you—"

"Cliff, for heaven's sake." She squeezed his arm. "You don't have to protect me. I can take it."

He looked into her eyes and recognized the strength there. "Just like you can take the violence of a car wreck."

"Yes."

He nodded. "Then I'd love you to come back to his room with me. Can I wait for you, or is fierce Dr. Edwards lurking around?"

Sarah chuckled. "He doesn't have emergency-room duty this morning. Give me a moment to change." She glanced at the side of Cliff's head, where hair was beginning to grow in the shaved patch where his wound had been. "You seem to be healing nicely."

"I had excellent care for the first twenty-four hours." He held her gaze. "I've missed you, Sarah."

"Cliff—"

"Go change. We'll talk later."

With a nod Sarah left him in the waiting room. As she fumbled with her jeans and pale blue shirt, she told herself they had nothing to discuss. Nothing about their own relationship, anyway. Naturally she wanted to offer support where his father was concerned.

Later, as they walked down the brightly lit hallway to his father's room, Cliff elaborated on the older man's condition. "He's become more than Mom can handle, but he's not sick enough to stay in a hospital full-time. We're looking at an intermediate care facility, although Mom hates to let go. I convinced her to allow me to bring him in this morning, but she'll be here any minute, I'm sure."

"I can understand why she'd cling to him, Cliff, after all their years together. But his care must be draining her."

He grimaced. "It is. I've tried to hire private nurses, but Mom complains that they invade her privacy."

"She's been doing everything for him?"

"Yes."

"Have you thought of the shock to her if she doesn't have that responsibility one day? What if he has to be institutionalized?"

"Shock?" Cliff looked puzzled. "I assumed she'd be relieved."

"Maybe, but she would have some empty hours with nothing to fill them."

"I suppose she'll go back to her charity work, then."

Sarah started to speak, then thought better of it. She would be out of line to suggest what Cora Hamilton should do with her spare time. And yet how foolish for Cliff to sacrifice himself to a business he disliked when perhaps his mother— But it wasn't Sarah's affair.

"Here it is. I'll go in first." Cliff pushed gently on the half-open door and walked into the dim room. "Dad, I've brought an old high school friend of mine to see you. Sarah Melton. She and I were in the history club together."

Sarah stepped into the room. As her eyes adjusted to the lack of light, she could see the gaunt man lying in the bed, but he bore almost no resemblance to the Jack Hamilton she remembered. Hair once neatly parted and combed was tangled and far too long for a man of Jack Hamilton's conservative tastes. Hands that had firmly clasped those of business tycoons and politicians now trembled and plucked at the rumpled white sheets.

"I don't recall your name, young man," he said to Cliff. "Are you a doctor?"

Sarah glanced at Cliff and saw him stiffen against the pain of not being recognized by his own father. "Mr. Hamilton, this is Cliff, your son. The light's not very good in here so you may not have seen him clearly."

"Cliff? Oh, Cliff. Well, well. How's college?"

"Fine, Dad."

The old man looked at Sarah. "You in college, too?"

"No, Mr. Hamilton. I work here at TMC."

"Mmm. Cliff's studying history. Won't make any money at it, though."

"Probably not, Dad."

"Say, would one of you send my secretary in? Time to stop jabbering and get to work. I bet she's out there doing her nails."

"I'll get her, Dad." Cliff motioned to Sarah, and they walked out the door together.

"And tell her to bring a thick notepad!" the old man called after them. "I've got important letters to dictate today."

"Good God," Cliff muttered, shaking his head.

"It must be very hard for you and your mother."

Cliff nodded and shoved both hands into his pockets as he walked. "Thanks for coming, Sarah. It sure helps not to face that alone." He paused at the nurses' station. "Dad asked for his secretary. I don't know if he needs anything, but maybe someone should check him."

"Will do, Mr. Hamilton," a short woman with a wide smile assured him.

"I'll walk this lady to her car, and I'll be back."

"Fine. No rush."

"Cliff, I can—"

He took Sarah's elbow. "Humor me. I need to be with you a little longer."

"Okay."

"And besides, I haven't asked what I came to the emergency room to ask."

Sarah glanced at him apprehensively. "What's that?"

"I'm taking the afternoon off tomorrow—from Dad, from work, from everything. How would you like to go on a picnic?"

"I thought I explained about that, Cliff. I'll do anything to help you with your father, but more than that..."

"You're a cruel tease, Sarah Jane. You bewitch me, give me a heady taste of your lovemaking, then turn me away. I'm suffering, lady."

"I'm sorry, but I know what's best. You don't belong in my world, and I don't belong in yours."

"You're going to make me beg, aren't you?"

"Don't do that, Cliff."

"Why not?"

She turned to him in frustration. "Because then I'll probably say yes, and that would be wrong."

He took hold of her shoulders. "Sarah, I beg you to spend tomorrow afternoon with me. I'm a desperate man."

Looking into his eyes was a mistake. She knew it and yet... "All right."

"You won't be sorry. I'll pick you up at noon, and I'll bring the food."

"Noon," she repeated like a hypnotized robot. "I'll be ready."

"You'll have to give me your address."

She complied, and he smiled gently. "It'll be okay, Sarah. We've got a few mountains to convert to mole-hills."

8

SARAH DIDN'T LOOK a second time when the aging pickup turned the corner and headed down her street. Certainly Cliff would be in a sports car. Shifting her weight on the concrete porch steps in front of her apartment, she bent to retie a dangling shoelace. When the truck door slammed, she glanced up, and her brown eyes widened.

"Cliff?"

"Come on, Sarah. It's only been one day. You can't have forgotten what I look like that fast."

She stood up in confusion. "Where did you get that truck?"

"It's Dad's." A straw cowboy hat cast speckled shade over the bronzed planes of his face. "But I've used it for years as a getaway truck."

"A what?"

"When life seems a little overwhelming, I climb in that old truck and drive into the desert somewhere. I've done it ever since I was sixteen."

"Alone?"

"Usually."

"Oh." Sarah thought of all the times she'd done the same sort of thing.

"What's the matter?" He hooked his thumbs in the worn pockets of his jeans. "Stereotype slipping?"

She grinned sheepishly. "Maybe."

He smiled back. "Good. Let's go."

Sarah retrieved her canvas tote bag from the front stoop and walked toward the truck with Cliff. No doubt about it, she was taken aback by the knowledge that he sometimes drove this old truck, wore jeans and faded plaid shirts and cherished moments alone in the desert. Even more important, he'd chosen to include her in today's "getaway." Cliff Hamilton was becoming very hard to resist.

When they reached the street, he opened the passenger's door and boosted her into the cab. His hands were firm and efficient at her waist. He released her immediately and closed the door after her with swift finality.

His nonchalance as he swung up into the driver's seat made her wonder if that brief body contact had affected him at all. His hands closing around her waist had set up a turmoil that even now had her clutching the armrest to keep from cuddling next to him on the wide bench seat.

As he coaxed the aging motor to life and manipulated the floor shift with precision, she realized he *had* driven this truck hundreds of times. The knowledge comforted her, even as the flexed muscles in his forearm when he shifted gears sent a thrill of sexual awareness charging through her.

"You wore your hair down again. Thanks, Sarah."

"Probably impractical for a picnic."

"Not if your date is crazy about it that way."

Sarah glanced away in confusion. She still wasn't used to extravagant compliments from him. "Have you—did you pick a spot for the picnic?"

"Sort of. Why?"

"I understood what you meant, about escaping from everything once in a while, and I, um, wondered if you'd like to see where I go when life becomes overwhelming."

His glance was warm. "I'd love it."

"Then take the Florence Highway toward Catalina."

"You've got it."

Sarah found it difficult not to watch him, this new Cliff Hamilton. In all her fantasies, he'd been an unattainable sophisticate in designer clothes and sleek cars. She'd never imagined him looking like a bronzed cowhand.

As if he could feel her attention on him, he took his eyes from the busy traffic for a second. "You don't know how close I came to sending you a dozen roses this week."

A dozen roses. Now *that* wouldn't have surprised her at all. The gesture fit the Cliff Hamilton she thought she knew. "But you didn't," she prompted.

"I rehashed our many conversations and realized roses, no, but a picnic, yes."

Her heart thumped faster. He'd obviously spent time analyzing their relationship, and instead of deciding they were hopelessly mismatched as she had, he'd considered where they could be on common ground. Cliff Hamilton didn't give up easily. Did she? Why should she automatically assume she couldn't fit into Cliff's life? Perhaps she'd been too hasty on Sunday, but thanks to Cliff's persistence, she'd have another chance.

"I'm glad you invited me, Cliff."

"Is that why you're hugging the door handle?"

"Uh..."

"You know, Sarah, I've never outgrown the thrill of tooling down the road with a beautiful woman nestled against my hip." He stretched his bronzed arm across the back of the seat, but his hand fell just short of touching her. "Red Rover, Red Rover, send Sarah on over," he murmured.

"Are you sure it won't interfere with your—"

Cliff groaned, rolling his eyes. "Lord, spare me from coy women. Do you, or do you not, want to touch me?"

Sarah blushed and laughed. "I do," she admitted, maneuvering around the gearshift and sliding into the curve of his arm. As her hip and thigh brushed his and his arm tightened around her shoulders, she almost expected to hear a sizzle, like a hot iron on damp cloth.

Instead, the air filled with a soft sigh, and she honestly didn't know whose it was.

"That's better," Cliff said, squeezing her arm gently.

"Mmm-hmm." Sarah couldn't have elaborated if her life had depended on it; the sensation of being close enough to feel him breathe, to feel his muscles contract as he settled himself more firmly against her, overcame her power of speech.

"You're in charge of shifting." He glanced down with a half smile. "Remember how to coordinate with someone else on the clutch?"

"I don't know. It's been a long time." She thought of Duane's old truck, remembered riding home after a drive-in movie and shifting for him so that they could maintain that magic connection between them. And all through that time of going steady with Duane, Sarah had pretended he was Cliff.

"Dig into your torrid past, Marvelous Melton. I can't believe you graduated from high school without learning this basic skill. Okay, here we go. Third gear."

Sarah watched Cliff's foot press the clutch, and she thrust the knob straight up, then winced as metal ground against metal.

"Too soon," Cliff said and shoved the clutch to the floor. "Now."

Sarah grasped the smooth wooden knob and pushed as Cliff eased the truck around the curve and up the ramp before he accelerated again.

"Okay, now Fourth," Cliff directed, and this time

Sarah watched his foot go all the way to the rubber mat before she pulled the floor shift toward her. The truck moved without a grumble into the right-hand lane.

"Aha! We did it," Sarah chortled.

"I knew you'd remember." Cliff pulled her closer. "It's like riding a bicycle or like..." He paused and rubbed his hand sensuously up and down her arm. "Something else I could mention."

Sarah drew a sharp breath.

"Do I detect a response to that remark?" Cliff chided. "Sarah, you've got goose bumps."

"You're tickling me."

"Tickled people don't get goose bumps. They giggle. Come on. Admit you've thought about Sunday."

"All right. I have."

"Can you admit what happened was pretty nice?"

Sarah gulped. Nice? That hardly described her memory of his lovemaking or the taut spring of desire he was winding ever tighter with his lazy caress. "Yes, it was."

"I'm glad you think so, too, Sarah, because I haven't been able to forget you or anything that we shared. I couldn't let you walk away."

"Oh."

"And I had to know whether Sunday had anything close to the effect on you that it had on me."

"I...guess it did." For a moment she was silent, digesting the amazing fact that he wanted her. Despite the evidence, the reality that he found her desirable still astonished her. Cliff Hamilton wanted Sarah Melton.

"That's encouraging. Would you like some music?"

"Sure." Sarah turned the radio on, and when a Ricky Scaggs tune blared out, she moved the red needle down the row of numbers.

"What was wrong with that station?"

"You don't like country music, do you?" Then she thought about his outfit today. "You do like country music. That's why the radio was tuned to KCUB."

"That's right. But you're in this cab, too. You have a vote."

"Ricky Scaggs is one of my favorites," she said, returning the needle to its original position. They listened in comfortable silence until the song ended. "You're handing me a few surprises today, Cliff. Unless you're putting me on..." She said it gently. She didn't want to insinuate that there was anything dishonest in his behavior, but she still had trouble believing this casually dressed country boy was Cliff Hamilton.

"I'll admit I steered away from country music and jeans when I was in college. I spent a lot of time at Harvard convincing people we had indoor plumbing in Arizona. I didn't need the added handicap of a ten-gallon hat and a leather belt with my name stamped on the back."

Sarah laughed. "I have a belt like that." Dolly Parton's high, sweet voice poured from the radio, and

Sarah wondered if she'd ever felt more relaxed and happy in her life.

"Me, too. But I left it off today, in case you'd think I was overdoing the image."

"The belt might have been a little obvious." She shifted gears at the stoplight. "I forgot that by taking this route we'd pass your office."

"Mmm-hmm." Cliff glanced at her. "You have been keeping track, haven't you?"

"I couldn't very well miss the gigantic letters on the building, could I? And every other For Sale sign on Oracle Road property has your name on it."

"Don't remind me. This is my day to ignore those signs."

"You're really not happy with real estate, are you?"

"It's okay. Face it, Sarah. How many of us get exactly what we want in life?"

"Not many, I guess." She remembered the sale of her family's land. "But you used to be so excited about history."

"Still am. When everything's more resolved with Dad—in other words when he's in some place where they can care for him—I might go back to graduate school part-time, or apply for an evening teaching assignment at Pima College."

"Good idea." Sarah smiled. "If you decide to teach, maybe I'll sign up for the course."

"I'd better warn you. In your case, I'd assign all sorts

of homework. You'd need private tutoring from the professor on a regular basis."

"Sounds...rigorous."

"I think you'd find the work satisfying, Miss Melton. You always did enjoy a challenge, as I recall."

"That's true." Sarah laughed happily. "What a beautiful day for a picnic."

Cliff dropped a quick kiss on her nose. "Isn't it, though? Well, damn. One more red light."

"That's okay. I have this shifting down pat." Sarah moved the gearshift into First as the truck halted at the intersection.

Cliff's gaze moved over her in warm assessment. "By George, I think she's got it."

Sarah felt kissed all over. "I had a good teacher."

Slowly Cliff bent his head, and she lifted her face to meet his. She felt his warm breath, and her body stirred in anticipation. At the first touch of velvet softness against her lips, she swayed dizzily. She was so hungry for him, so hungry.

The horn bleating behind them nearly tumbled her off the seat, but Cliff's strong arms shot out and held her steady.

"Oh!" she cried in sudden embarrassment. "I completely forgot where we—"

"Don't lose your place," Cliff admonished, disentangling himself and stepping on the accelerator. "I'll have us out of this traffic jam in a jiffy."

Sarah glanced in the rearview mirror and prayed

that the occupants of the foreign compact behind them weren't people she—or Cliff—knew. She understood now why lovers longed for their own desert island. In her case she had the next best thing, her own private desert. At least until the sale went through.

"Okay, we're officially on the Florence Highway. How far are we going?"

"Just a few more miles. There's a dirt road to the right."

"Most of that's private property, as I recall. We aren't about to trespass, are we, Sarah Jane?"

"No. The land belongs to my parents, an inheritance from my great-grandfather."

"The pocket watch great-grandfather?"

"Those were his only two legacies. A watch and a ten-acre homestead."

"Anything on it?"

"Not anymore. My folks always dreamed of building a house, but they could never afford it. And now..."

"Now what?" he prodded gently.

"Dad's been a miner all his life, but he's decided to retrain for a career in computers. They're selling some of the land to pay for his schooling."

Cliff fell silent. He could tell how much the property meant to her from the way she talked about it. Hell, she'd admitted that this was where she came to recover from life's bumps and bruises. His first instinct was to buy the land himself and find some way to turn it over to her, but he bit back the words. If she came unglued over one lousy dress, what would happen with a piece of property worth several thousand dollars?

"Who's selling it?"

"Al Hollencraft. They wanted to give the business to a Catalina real-estate company first. If Hollencraft doesn't sell it, they'll contact a Tucson company."

"Which could be us." What irony.

"Yes, I suppose. Turn at the next road."

"Good thing I brought the truck," Cliff said between bounces as they navigated the rough road.

"Grading costs money, too. Besides, I'm about the only one who comes out here anymore. Over there, Cliff. See the big paloverde and that huge saguaro? There's a level spot to park, in the shade of the tree."

"Wow. Look at the yellow blooms on that baby. Must be a blue paloverde. Nothing more gorgeous in the world." He glanced at her. "Amend that. Nothing more gorgeous in the plant world."

"You're a smooth talker, Cliff Hamilton."

"No, you're a beautiful sight on this spring day, Sarah Melton. I'm stating the obvious." He parked the truck and gazed down at her. "And unless we get out of this truck and eat our picnic lunch immediately, I'm going to start kissing you, and all my efforts to provide food will be wasted."

Excitement curled through Sarah. "Heaven forbid," she said breathlessly, wiggling out of his arms and opening her door. "Let's eat."

"I was afraid you'd suggest that."

Moments later they were sitting on the truck's tailgate, unwrapping sandwiches and sipping wine.

"I can see why you come to this place when the going gets rough, Sarah." Cliff took off his hat and laid it on the truck bed. "I love the quiet."

"Me, too." She swallowed a bite of sandwich and looked at Cliff. "Bologna?"

"You expected caviar?"

"As a matter of fact."

"The wine's imported. Very pricey. How's that?"

"Imported wine and bologna?"

He nodded. "Part of my not-so-subtle attempt to reduce those mountains to molehills."

"Oh."

"You see, I like caviar," he admitted, taking another sip from his plastic wineglass. "And expensive cheese and exotic fruit. I also like bologna and tuna fish and macaroni. I'm not a snob, Sarah. We can get along. Believe me."

Sarah looked down at the tender green of the wild grass sprouting beneath their feet. Springtime. A time for new beginnings. For changing old preconceptions. She swung her legs back and forth. "I've been pretty thickheaded, haven't I?"

Cliff grinned. "If you insist."

"Sort of a reverse snobbery, in a way."

"Something like that."

"It must have been the city air that caused me to be so dense. I always think better out here."

"And what do you think, Sarah Jane?"

She glanced up shyly. "I think I'm very lucky to be with you today."

"That's nice. Anything else?"

"Yes. We're more alike than I thought."

"That's it?"

She put down her wineglass and turned to him. "No. I think if you don't kiss me in the next two seconds, I'll expire on the spot."

"Lady," he said, putting aside his glass, "I like the way you think."

His arms came around her as naturally as if they'd been kissing on tailgates for years. His lips, flavored with white wine, unerringly found hers. Cushioning her head with his arm, Cliff eased her back on the truck bed as his kiss became more demanding.

She felt his shoulder muscles ripple under his soft cotton shirt. As his hips pressed into hers, she longed for much more than a kiss from him.

He lifted his head, and she gazed dreamily into his blue, blue eyes. Behind his head the green branches of the paloverde were bursting with tiny yellow flowers. The air smelled crisp and new; the sun warmed them as they lay on the scratched metal truck bed. Sarah framed Cliff's face with loving hands and smiled. He had become a part of her world.

"Sarah, you know I want you."

"Yes."

"I can feel your heartbeat. You want me, too."

"Yes."

"But I don't want to make love to you here, beautiful as it is. Someone might happen along." He wove his fingers through her copper hair. "Come home with me, Sarah Jane."

9

"To your house?" Sarah frowned.

"It really isn't far, and I'd like you to see it."

Sarah's sense of well-being began to disappear. Cliff fit beautifully into her world of warm desert springtime, casual clothes and pickup trucks. She might not slip so easily into his extravagant life-style, however.

"Where is it?"

"Just off Skyline Drive."

She could have guessed that. "I, ah, suppose it's pretty big, huh?"

Cliff sighed. "It's palatial. The Cleveland Indians use my living room for spring training, and Olympic swimmers train in my bathtub. Is that about what you expected?"

"You think I'm being overly sensitive again."

"You? Never."

"I just wonder if I wouldn't feel uncomfortable."

He sighed again in exasperation. "It's just a house, Sarah. Don't be intimidated by the damn house."

"Okay."

"You are! It's still there in your voice. With no good reason, I might add. I have never once bragged about my house or my money or any of my material possessions."

"That's true."

"But, damn it, I won't apologize for them, either."

"You shouldn't have to."

"No, I shouldn't."

She traced the angry lines around his mouth and watched them soften at her touch. Slowly the sparks of irritation faded from his eyes, and desire smoldered again. Sarah took a deep breath. "Does your offer still stand?"

"You bet."

"Then I'd like to come to your house, Cliff."

"Thank you, Sarah, for taking a step toward me." He kissed her gently and helped her up. They stowed the picnic remains in the ice chest and were soon bouncing down the rutted dirt road toward the highway.

Once the truck turned onto smooth blacktop, Sarah scooted next to Cliff and rested her hand on his thigh. She felt the muscles flex at her touch, and he gathered her close.

"You don't know how much it means when you take the initiative, Sarah." His chest heaved. "God, I don't want you to be afraid of me or the life I lead. None of the trappings really matter. It's still just you and me."

"I'll try to remember that. I really will."

"Good." Cliff drove fast, scanning the roadside for police cars. Neither he nor Sarah spoke, both gripped by the need to retreat to a place where they could explore the passion surging between them.

After they'd turned left off Skyline Drive, Sarah began searching the gray-green hillsides for a house to fit her image, a structure that dominated the landscape and proclaimed the wealth and position of its owner.

Then, unexpectedly, the road veered to the right; the house appeared, almost as if it had grown up from the desert floor. The one-story, sand-colored dwelling looked more like molded sculpture than architecture. Except for three garage doors, Sarah couldn't see a single right angle. Desert landscaping camouflaged the house even more, and Sarah was surprised when the word "unpretentious" flashed into her mind.

Cliff reached in front of Sarah and took a plastic control box from the glove compartment. One of the doors buzzed open, and he pulled the truck into the dim interior of the garage and turned off the engine with a sigh.

"We're here," he said, shoving his thumb onto the button that brought the door down with a thump behind them.

"I can't see a thing," Sarah said, wondering if Cliff could hear the hammering of her heart.

"I'll guide you."

She felt his arm curve around her in the darkness and heard his hat scratch against the dashboard where he tossed it. Then his lips found her cheek, and she jumped.

"Kiss me, Sarah," he whispered, capturing her chin and bringing her closer.

Tentatively she softened her mouth against his. His sun-drenched scent mingled with the garage smells of car exhaust and power tools and the earthy scent of stored peat moss. With a soft moan he gathered her against him and delved deep into her mouth. His kiss was long and thorough, as if to remind her of the path they'd blazed together in the glow of a kerosene lamp.

When at last Cliff lifted his head, he was breathing hard. "A few days, but it feels like forever since I've held you like this," he said, nibbling at her bottom lip. "How did you become essential to me so fast?"

"I don't know," she murmured. "I never meant for things to—to go this far."

He chuckled. "I'm aware of that. You're as skittish as a jackrabbit." His hand slid up her rib cage to pass almost casually across her taut breast, and she gasped. "But skittish or not, you want me."

"Yes."

"At least I've got one thing in my favor. And I'm not going to be handicapped by a steering wheel and gas fumes. Come on." He opened the door, and the overhead light flashed on in the cab. Sarah blinked and looked up into Cliff's smiling face. "Your lips are rosy red. Who've you been kissing, Sarah Jane?"

"I'm not the kind of girl who'll kiss and tell, sir."

Cliff leaped to the garage floor and helped her from the cab. "I wish you were," he said, closing the door and plunging them into darkness again. "I wish you were so proud of what we've got going that you'd shout it to the world." When she didn't respond, he squeezed her shoulder. "Let's go see if the Cleveland Indians have vacated the living room yet."

Sarah decided Cliff hadn't exaggerated much. The garage door opened into a kitchen that could provide for a hotelful of guests. If the outside of Cliff's house was unpretentious, the inside made up for it.

Gleaming Italian tile floors occasionally gave way to thick scatter rugs positioned strategically in front of massive pieces of furniture; she suspected that they'd been hand carved in Mexico. As Sarah surveyed the curved bank of windows overlooking the city and the glass wall opposite with a view of the Catalinas, she tried to remember what he'd said—the trappings didn't matter.

"I hope you hold stock in Windex," she said brightly.

"They don't have to be washed as often as you might think because I don't have any little shavers around to put handprints all over them." He walked up behind Sarah and slipped his arms around her waist. "But don't interpret that to mean I'm against little shavers. How about you?"

"Cliff, I think we're being a little premature to discuss—"

"Oh? Why is that?"

"This is far too early to be considering a—a permanent commitment of some kind."

"Hmm." He nuzzled her ear. "You want to keep everything purely sexual, is that it?"

"No! I mean—I don't know what I mean."

"That's okay." The hands that had encircled her waist moved upward to cup her breasts. "A little confusion is allowed at a time like this," he murmured as his thumbs stroked her nipples to rigid attention. "I'm not the most clearheaded fellow in the world now, either."

Sarah moaned softly and leaned against him. "Your house is beautiful, Cliff."

"To hell with the house." His voice rumbled seductively in her ear as he pulled her shirt from the waistband of her jeans. "Only one part of it interests me at this moment." He stroked her bare skin and moved upward to unfasten the front clasp of her bra. "Let me show you the master bedroom."

She closed her eyes to savor the sensation of his fingers kneading her pliant flesh. Nothing mattered but his touch, the promise of another chance to make glorious love with him.

"Sarah," he murmured, his warm breath sending high-voltage signals from her sensitive earlobes to the rest of her body, "I'm taking you to bed."

She turned in his arms and gazed up at him, her eyelids heavy with desire. "No," she corrected softly. "We're going together."

Understanding glowed in his blue eyes, and a trace of a smile flitted across his face. "Much better," he said in a not-quite-steady voice.

Arms entwined around each other, they negotiated the wide hallway toward a double door.

"Take off your shoes," Cliff said, bending to untie his own. "You'll love walking barefoot. I just had this room redecorated."

Sarah glanced through the wide doorway and understood. Sunk two steps below the level of the rest of the house was the biggest bedroom and the widest bed Sarah had ever seen. Tile floors gave way to ivory plush carpet so thick that she cried out in pleasure as her toes sank into it. The comforter on the bed was the same shade as the rug, and the only color in the room came from blue and green throw pillows on the bed.

For one wonderful moment Sarah allowed herself to believe the fantasy, to believe she could be Cliff's wife, mistress of this enormous house, mother of their children. Her brown eyes shone with the joy of it, and Cliff, seeing the future in her face, caught his breath.

"Yes, Sarah. We can have it all. Everything." He lowered his head to taste her lips, and she raised her mouth trustingly to him. He marveled at how right it felt, holding her close in this room—almost as if he'd had her in mind when he'd chosen the new decorating scheme a few weeks earlier.

Gently he pulled her knit shirt up until he had to relinquish her lips to lift it over her head. Her hair was

caught up at first in the collar of the shirt and then fell
free in shimmering red-gold waves down her back. He
pushed her bra down over her arms and tossed both
garments in a heap on the ivory carpet before turning
back to her.

She stood proudly before him, breasts thrust forward, the tan outline of her bikini top more pronounced in the sunlit bedroom than it had been in the
dim glow of a kerosene lamp. Under his gaze her nipples tightened, and his hand moved forward involuntarily.

"Do you know how exquisite you are?"

"I know you make me feel that way."

"God, how I love looking at you, touching you."

"It works two ways, Cliff," she breathed, catching
his hand and lowering it to his side. "Fair is fair." For
the first time in her life, she wanted to tease and entice
a man, to aggressively arouse him, seduce him.

Her breasts quivered as she unbuttoned his shirt and
pulled it from his jeans. Deliberately she moved forward and brushed lazily against him. As she watched
his piercing blue eyes become slumberous with desire,
she felt a moment of triumph. No matter what happened after today, she would remember that look in
his eyes that told her his need blocked out rational
thought, that he would sacrifice anything to make love
to her.

Giddy with power, she bent her head to swirl her
tongue past his coarse mahogany chest hair and cap-

ture his nipple between her teeth. His muffled groan encouraged her, and her fingers went boldly to the buckle of his belt as her tongue and teeth continued their assault on his restraint. The belt was easy, and then one by one the metal fasteners of his jeans surrendered to her capable fingers.

Taunting him with her eyes, she hooked one finger inside the waistband of his briefs and moved it slowly back and forth. When he caught his breath, she laughed low in her throat and moved her hand to caress the throbbing fullness of him through the confining cotton. She repeated the light movement, and he groaned and caught her hand.

"Fair is fair," he said hoarsely. "And you're ahead."

"Ah, and Cliff Hamilton's not used to that," she purred as she pulled her hand away from his and ran her fingernails across his bare chest.

"I think you should be in the same condition." He paused, breathing hard. "Sarah, you're driving me—"

"Crazy? Good." Her hand moved seductively back down to his thigh, then inched higher, and the warm pulsing she felt beneath her fingers made her tremble with desire.

"Enough, woman," he rasped, gripping her hand with steely determination.

Sarah's laugh was rich with passion. "Is this the part where you swing me into your arms and carry me to the bed?"

"Not with a vixen like you," he breathed, nudging

her backward. "I'm saving my strength to humble you into submission, wench."

The edge of the mattress caught Sarah behind her knees, and she tumbled backward onto the fluffy comforter. Her eyes widened as Cliff dispensed with briefs and jeans in one swift movement that revealed the rigid evidence of his desire. Primitive passion flared in his blue eyes as he grabbed for the waistband of her jeans, and instinctively she moved away, both aroused and intimidated by the sight of him.

Immediately his hand stilled in the act of unsnapping her jeans, and his eyes sought hers. "Too fast, Sarah?" he accused almost gruffly, and his eyes searched hers questioningly. "I guess so."

With a sigh he sank gently to the bed beside her, although all his senses screamed for him to rip the clothes from her body and demand relief from her sweet torture. Did she realize how her touch had stoked the need that raged in him until he ached? That controlling his urges now was making him quiver with unslaked sexual thirst?

"You startled me," she said softly.

"Sarah," he began, and his hand shook as he cupped her face, "all that playing around you did really turned me on, and all I could think of was getting the rest of our clothes off and taking you, perhaps even taking you a little roughly, a little fiercely. You didn't expect that, did you?"

"I—I guess not."

The corner of his mouth turned up ruefully. "You've got a powerful weapon, lady, and I think you need some lessons in how to use it."

"Cliff, I'm sorry. I—"

He interrupted her with a long, lingering kiss. "It's okay, Sarah Jane. We'll begin with lesson one. Pay attention." Gently he urged her back on the ivory comforter and planted light kisses down her neck and along her collarbone. Gradually his lips came closer and closer to the tingling peak of each breast, then retreated. She whimpered, wanting all the sensations he could give her, and he smiled against her skin. "Pay attention, Sarah," he repeated.

He began making small forays with his tongue, circling temptingly close to each tight bud but never touching either one. Sarah writhed in frustration against the smooth comforter until at last, with a groan, she wound her fingers through Cliff's hair and pulled him roughly against her. "Please," she whispered urgently. As his tongue and lips at last granted her wish, she arched her back and sighed in satisfaction.

Just before his mouth came back to cover hers, he murmured, "End of lesson one," and she felt his hand unfasten her jeans. Lifting himself away from her, he pulled off both her jeans and panties, then settled himself beside her again.

"Did you learn anything from lesson one?" he asked, his own reined-in passion flickering in his eyes.

"Perhaps," she murmured, her body growing hot under his purposeful gaze.

"I think you need lesson two." His head dipped to capture her lips again while his fingers stroked lightly along her inner thigh. He created lazy circles, spiraling ever upward on her soft skin. When he reached the top of her thigh, he brushed across the triangle of golden hair and continued the slow spiral down to the back of her knee. He changed his touch to a light massage but each time stopped just short of her heated core, and at last she began to moan softly and twist her hips from side to side.

Releasing her mouth, he slid down her body and feathered the inside of each thigh with his tongue and lips. She felt the warmth of him coming closer, and the molten ache inside her became almost unbearable. But all he bestowed was the warmth of his breath as he kissed the pale skin at the top of her thigh—and stopped.

Her nails bit into his shoulders. "Cliff, I want you," she cried out hoarsely.

"Don't you want to play anymore?" he asked, sliding up beside her. His fingers trailed up her thigh to touch her intimately this time, and she gasped her answer. "No!"

"Wanting like this makes you feel a little wild, doesn't it, Sarah?" he said hoarsely as he teased and stroked her to fever pitch.

"Cliff!"

"Don't forget how you feel right now, Sarah, because that's what you do to a man when you seduce him. He becomes a little wild, and he may move quickly because he needs you so much—"

"Love me, Cliff, now," she begged desperately.

"Gladly, my darling." But still he took his time, and when she felt him slowly enter her, she grasped his hips and pulled him deep inside with a fierce little cry.

"Oh, Sarah, I think you've learned your lesson," Cliff moaned and unleashed the fever of his own passion to bury himself in her again and again, mingling his cries with hers in the ivory newness of the haven he had created, unknowingly, just for them.

Afterward Sarah lay quietly listening to the sounds around her—Cliff's even breathing, the noisy chatter of a cactus wren outside the window, the faraway sound of a car's engine. Lying in this magnificent ivory room, she could hardly imagine that at eleven tonight she'd be back in the emergency room X-raying patients. And what would Cliff be doing? Sipping an after-dinner liqueur? Watching a movie on the wide-screen television she knew must be hidden somewhere in this fabulous house?

No doubt about it—the house made her painfully aware of her poverty. After an afternoon in Cliff's perfectly appointed bedroom, she'd be ashamed to take him into the tiny room where she slept on a lumpy double bed with a laminated headboard.

Encouraging this madness between them was the

most foolish thing she'd ever done, she acknowledged, turning her head and gazing lovingly at his sleeping face, his tousled hair and the square patch of prickly new growth where his head had been shaved. They were wrong for each other, but how could she ever leave him?

The noise of the car engine became more pronounced, and Sarah wondered with the beginnings of panic if someone could be coming to the house. Then she heard the crunch of tires on gravel and reached over quickly to shake Cliff's shoulder.

"I think someone's here," she whispered as his eyelids fluttered open.

"Who?" he asked sleepily.

She smiled. "How should I know? I don't live here. But I heard a car, and—"

Her assertion was confirmed by footsteps on the brick walkway and the deep chime of the doorbell. Even the doorbell sounds classy, Sarah thought as she scrambled to find her clothes.

"Don't worry. Probably just a salesman," Cliff mumbled, shoving his legs into his jeans. "Don't get dressed, Sarah. We still have time...."

What he intended to do with that time she had to imagine because he left hurriedly to answer the door. In spite of his request, she got completely dressed except for her shoes, which were lined up beside his outside the bedroom door.

Whoever the caller was, he or she was inside the

house now; Sarah heard the front door close before the conversation continued. The visitor was a woman. "I shouldn't have bothered you on your day off, but his request upset me so that I came by without thinking," she said clearly.

"That's okay. But I'd better warn you I'm not alone."

Sarah froze. *Thanks a lot, Cliff.*

There was a moment of silence before the woman spoke again. "A girl? Cliff, I'm sorry. But you've never brought anyone here, so I—I'll leave."

"No, don't go. I want you to meet her. You will sooner or later, anyway, and we might as well get the awkward part out of the way. Just a minute."

As his feet whispered toward her across the Italian tile, Sarah contemplated climbing out a window and hitchhiking home. How could he do this to her? Who on earth was he dragging her out to meet, and how could she face whoever it was, who could no doubt imagine exactly what they'd been doing for the past hour?

Cliff appeared in the double doorway looking sheepish. "Good, you're dressed," he said in an undertone. "Could you come out for a little while?"

"Cliff, this is embarrassing!" Sarah protested softly.

"I know, but I'm kind of glad it happened." He crossed the ivory carpet to pull her to her feet.

"Who's here?"

"My mother."

10

CLIFF'S ANSWER paralyzed Sarah's vocal cords.

"Please, Sarah. Believe me, meeting her is the best way out of an uncomfortable situation. We can all handle it."

"Easy for you to say."

"No, it's not. I've never been in this situation with my mother before. But I don't like sneaking around. You're not that type, either, so let's face the music."

Sarah paused a moment longer, then nodded like a mechanical toy and walked out of the bedroom. She imagined her face could double for a stoplight.

A tiny woman with carefully coiffed gray hair and a golden tan turned from the large windows overlooking the mountains. Her silken blouse and navy skirt exuded style; diamonds winked from her earlobes and fingers.

"Hello, Mrs. Hamilton."

"Mom, you remember Sarah Melton. She and I belonged to the high school history club, and you've met her a few times at TMC, I think. She's in the X-ray department."

"Of course." Cora Hamilton smiled and held out her hand.

Sarah extended a sweating palm and returned the brief handshake. She doubted that the older woman remembered her at all, but Cora had impeccable manners and would pretend they were fond acquaintances.

"Sarah was my lifesaver in the emergency room last weekend. We hadn't seen each other since high school, and we've been catching up on each other's lives."

Sarah struggled to think of an appropriate comment to fill the silence. Cliff had been giving her a tour of the house? Barefoot? She shot a look of appeal in his direction and noticed his shirt was buttoned unevenly.

Cora followed the direction of Sarah's horrified gaze, and a smile touched her perfectly outlined lips. "Sorry, kids. Next time I'll call."

"Oh, that won't be necessary," Sarah began. "We won't—"

"Good idea, Mom."

"Nice to meet you, Sarah. I'll be in touch later, Cliff." Cora picked up her purse from the couch.

"Wait." Cliff touched her arm. "Tell me about this party business."

His mother's gaze swept over him, and she began to chuckle. "Cliff, dear, if I'm going to have a conversation with you without rolling on the floor, you'll have to rebutton your shirt."

He glanced down and grinned. "Oh."

Cora laughed as he took her suggestion. "In my own

defense, Sarah, lest you think I'm an insensitive mother, I didn't know Cliff was currently...involved."

Cliff finished his task and put an arm around Sarah. "As a matter of fact, I'm very much involved. That's why I dragged her out here, knowing she'd cheerfully shoot me for it. I couldn't have her lurking in the background as if we had something to be ashamed of."

"Goodness, I should hope not. You're almost thirty, and I'd begun to worry this past year that you'd let the business ruin your social life. I'm glad to know it hasn't."

"Sarah means a little more to me than social life, Mom."

"I'm glad of that, too. You've needed someone special to come along."

"Cliff, you shouldn't give your mother the wrong impression. Mrs. Hamilton, we're not—"

"Cora, dear. Call me Cora. And you don't need to explain anything right now."

"But—"

"Tell us about the party, Mom," Cliff inserted tactfully.

"The party. Oh, yes." The sprightly expression vanished from her face. "Cliff, I came over here, causing this embarrassment to poor Sarah, because I just don't know what to do about your father."

Cliff left Sarah's side and guided his mother to the couch. "What's wrong?"

Sarah watched their interaction, observed how Cora

became more uncertain and how Cliff immediately rushed to the rescue.

Cora twisted her hands in her lap. "At the hospital this afternoon, your father decided his birthday was coming up, which it isn't, but you know how mixed up he is. Anyway, he demanded a big party. No gifts—you know how we used to do it—donations to charity instead. What should I do, Cliff?"

Cliff frowned. "Don't worry. I'll think of something."

"He wants me to invite all our old friends, as well as the kids who were part of your crowd, Cliff. I'm at a loss."

Sarah asked the question without thinking. "Why not have the party?"

Cora's penciled eyebrows rose, and she glanced at her son. "Does Sarah know about your father?"

"I took her to see him yesterday morning."

"Then you realize, Sarah, that a huge party would be ludicrous under the circumstances. Cliff has convinced me to move Jack to some type of rest home, possibly within a few weeks."

"I think that's an even stronger reason to have the party."

"Sarah may be right, Mom."

"Oh, I don't know. Most of our friends don't know how bad he's become in the past few months. I'd hate to burden them with—"

"Hey, Mom. They all shared the good times, and I'll

bet money they're willing to share the bad, if you'll let them. Let's give Dad his party."

Cora was silent for a moment, then looked down at the floor and dabbed furtively at one eye. "I suppose it is only fitting. That he go out with a bang."

"Absolutely," Cliff agreed. "We'll do it right—caterers, champagne, string quartet, house decorated. I'll help. And if Sarah's game, I'd like her to come, too."

"Oh, no, I—"

Cora glanced up. "Why, of course you'll come, dear. After all, it was your idea to grant his wish. And you're both right. Jack deserves this, and we'll do it, even if we're the only three who accept the invitation."

"Don't worry, Mom. Everyone will show. They're good people."

"That's true." Cora took a deep breath and consulted her gold wristwatch. "I'd better go home and start planning. Might as well make it a week from Saturday night. Jack will be finished with his hospital tests by then, and he'll be home, at least temporarily, until we finish the arrangements for...the other arrangements."

"Sounds good to me," Cliff said quickly to cover his mother's distress. "Are you free a week from Saturday, Sarah?"

"I work this weekend, so yes, I'll be free."

"Wonderful." Cora Hamilton smiled bravely. "As a matter of fact, I'll have fun organizing a party again. I'm pretty good at that, you know, once somebody makes the decision for me. It's been a pleasure, Sarah, and I look forward to seeing you again next Saturday."

"Thank you...Cora."

"That's better." She patted Sarah's arm. "And, Cliff, I'll talk to you tomorrow."

"I'll check on Dad before I go to the office," Cliff said, opening the heavy wooden door for his mother. Carefully he closed the door after her and turned to Sarah with a broad smile.

"You're terrific," he said. "The party's a wonderful idea, and finally Mom will have something to plan again. I saw the sparkle in her eyes when she left. It's been a long time since she's looked that excited about something."

"Cliff..." Sarah hesitated, then plunged on. "Your mother's quite a talented lady."

"Of course she is."

"Do you ever wonder if she's...had a real chance to grow, to explore her potential?" *Go easy, Sarah.*

"What do you mean, explore her potential? She doesn't have a particularly carefree life with my dad in his present condition. I don't think she's worried about exploring her potential right now."

"What about in a few weeks? What will happen then?"

"She'll find plenty to do. She always does."

"But, Cliff, why should she just *find* something? Why not ask her to get involved in Hamilton Realty?"

"In business? You've got to be kidding. That's a tough world. They'd eat her alive."

"You just agreed she's talented."

"She is in some ways, and certainly courageous. But that isn't all you need to succeed in business. You have to be aggressive, persistent, thick-skinned..."

"I think your mother might be capable of running that business, Cliff." *If you stop babying her.* "And when your father's in some sort of home, she'll be anxious for something to keep her busy."

"She has the charity work."

"Why? Why should she spend her time on volunteer work when she could take over Hamilton Realty and leave you free to teach history, like you always dreamed of doing?"

"Sarah, you don't understand. My mother is fifty-five years old. She's never worked at a regular job."

"The charity drives have taught her a lot, and she could learn the rest. Look at my father. He's retraining after all these years."

"But he's a—" Cliff stopped himself before he said it, but Sarah was already clenching her hands.

"But he's a man. Cliff Hamilton, you're a chauvinist."

"A realist," he countered. "My mother's never shown the slightest interest in real estate. And she leans on me for major decisions. You saw that."

"She leans because you allow it. And just because it

hasn't occurred to her that she might get involved doesn't make it a bad idea."

He shook his head. "I can't see it as a possibility."

Sarah bit her lip in frustration. She had no real right to push the matter in the first place. As she'd tried to tell Cora Hamilton, she and Cliff were just friends. Wonderful things happened when he held her, when they shut the world away and passion claimed them, but a commitment had to be based on more than that. This disagreement illustrated one more area in which they were miles apart.

He crossed the room and took her by the shoulders. "You're very quiet all of a sudden."

"Cliff, you've tried to prove we're compatible, but I'm afraid our differences are greater than you think."

"I can't accept that." He rubbed his hands up and down her arms. "Not after this afternoon. We're so good together, Sarah."

"A relationship needs more than sex."

"We have more than that. Don't try to reduce what happens between us to mere sex. You heard my mother. I've needed someone special. Someone like you, Sarah."

"Cliff, don't—"

"Listen to me. The desert's an unusual place. Seeds lie fallow for years, waiting for the right growing conditions. Ten years ago we were both too young. The conditions weren't right for a relationship to grow. But now—"

"Now the conditions are worse!" Sarah insisted. "You're entrenched in a world I've never known. We have different attitudes about how women should be treated."

"You seemed to enjoy how I treated you an hour ago."

"That's different."

"No, it's not. My attitude toward women is reflected in how I make love—cherishing, protecting, delighting in the differences between us."

"That's straight out of the nineteenth century!"

"Nevertheless, you responded."

"Yes." And she was doing it again.

"Don't try to tell me you don't like being cherished." He slid his hand over the curve of her cheek and threaded his fingers through her hair. "Don't tell me you don't like this." He bent his head and kissed her parted lips gently until she trembled against him.

Slowly he drew away and gazed deep into her brown eyes. "My heart's going a mile a minute, Sarah. That doesn't happen with every woman I meet. Not even every woman I kiss. I can't remember wanting someone like this—ever."

"Nor I," she whispered. "Heaven help me."

"You don't have to be at the hospital until eleven."

"No."

"Stay with me until then."

Sarah tried to remember all the reasons she had for walking out of Cliff's house and never coming back, but none of them made sense while her body ached like this. With a sigh she closed her eyes and pulled his head down to her waiting lips.

SLEEP BECAME a scarce commodity for Sarah during the next few days, but even without her normal hours of rest she felt charged with incredible energy, and she knew the source was Cliff's lovemaking.

Each morning after work she grabbed a quick nap before he picked her up early in the afternoon. They spent the remainder of each day together—sharing meals, taking walks and making love in Cliff's ivory bedroom. They couldn't get enough of each other, and by tacit consent they avoided discussing any subject that would cause controversy between them.

Sarah knew that they were living a fantasy, that the time must come when they would have to face their problems, but after each golden day in Cliff's arms, she longed for just one more. Only one more. At last, one evening as they lay entwined on Cliff's enormous bed, he admitted his business was suffering.

"I've got to spend all day tomorrow in the office, Sarah. If I could work when you do, everything would be fine, but my clients don't particularly want to hear from me at three o'clock in the morning."

"I wondered how you were managing to run Hamilton Realty and spend so much time with me. But I was afraid to ask."

Cliff pulled her head to his chest and stroked her

hair. "I wish I had nothing else to do but make love to you. Unfortunately, business is only part of it. My mother needs help with the party, and as you recall, I offered my services."

"I remember." *And we fought about your overprotectiveness. Do you remember that?*

"And I haven't seen as much of my dad as I should."

"I feel a little selfish, Cliff."

He hugged her gently. "Don't you dare. I've chosen to be with you because I can't help myself. These days have been like magic for me."

"Me, too."

"Hey, you won't know this, I bet. Who was secretary of state under Harrison?"

"You've got to come up with harder questions than that, Hamilton. Harrison's secretary of state was Daniel Webster."

Cliff chuckled. "Marvelous Melton does it again," he said, continuing to stroke her hair. "Sarah..."

She held her breath.

"I know that physically we've held nothing back in these few days, but I, for one, have been careful about what I've said."

She nodded against his chest. Maybe he did remember. "So have I. I didn't want to fight."

"Especially when loving is so much more fun. And that's what we've been doing, Sarah, even though I've never put a label on it."

He tipped her chin up and gazed into her eyes. "I've

been afraid I'd scare you, spoil what was happening between us." His blue eyes glowed with an intense fire. "But I won't be with you tomorrow, and I want to give you something to think about. I do love you, Sarah Jane Melton."

She let out her breath in a shuddering sigh, and tears misted her eyes.

"Don't cry. I'm very happy about it."

"So am I. That's why I'm crying."

"It is?"

"People in love cry a lot, didn't you know?"

"People like you?"

"Yes."

"Sarah…"

"Yes, yes, yes! I love you so much it hurts."

"Oh, God." He crushed her to him. "I didn't expect you to say that, and now I'm crying."

"What a pair," Sarah mumbled, sniffing.

"Damn right we are. Oh, Sarah. Sarah! You love me! Did you hear that, folks? Marvelous Melton loves me!"

As he shouted his delight, Sarah laughed through her tears. And then she thought, without wanting to, that there was no Ethel to pound on the wall when Cliff made noise in his house. They'd declared their love, but they'd discussed none of the differences between them. Would love be enough to see them through?

Two days later, as she stood facing an angry Cliff in his kitchen, she decided it wouldn't.

"What do you mean, you're not going to the party? Mom is counting on you. *I'm* counting on you, for God's sake."

"I can't afford it, Cliff. I found a dress on sale but then realized I didn't have the right shoes. Why is it important for me to go, anyway? No one there will know me."

"No one except the host, who can't imagine not having the woman he loves beside him. And I have a solution to the problem."

"No."

"Sarah, this is silly. It's because of me that you're going to the party. Why shouldn't I pay for your outfit?"

"I wouldn't feel right."

"Suppose we were married. Would you let your husband buy you a dress and shoes?"

"We're not married."

"Then let's fix that right quick. Consider yourself proposed to."

"Cliff! Don't be flip about something like that."

"I'm sorry if it sounded flip. I'm dead serious. Sarah, will you be my wife?"

She stared at him. "You mean it."

"Of course I mean it." He grabbed her hand and pulled her after him down the hall. "I have something in my desk drawer that should convince you how much I mean it. I intended to broach this subject a little later, but the time seems to be now."

He drew her into the room he used as a home office

and reached into his pocket for the key to his desk. Moments later he placed a black velvet box in her trembling hand.

"Open it."

She pried open the box. A graceful solitaire diamond ring glittered on its black velvet cushion.

"Share my life, Sarah. You've become the most important person in the world to me, and I love you more than you'll ever know."

She looked into his eyes, tears streaming down her cheeks. "Cliff, I'm not ready for this. We're not ready. Don't make me answer yet, please."

A shadow crossed his face, and he brushed the tears gently from her cheeks. "Not exactly the enthusiastic response I hoped for." He sighed. "But not a definite refusal, either."

"No, not a refusal. A—a rain check."

"A rain check." He smiled crookedly. "Okay. Then how the hell am I supposed to get you to Dad's party?"

"I guess we'll go shopping for a dress and shoes."

"Accepting an outfit is less dangerous than accepting a ring, is that it?"

"Something like that. Cliff, we have so many things to talk about before we make any commitment to each other."

"I can't imagine what we could say that would change my mind about you, so the reservations must be on your side."

"Apparently."

"Care to outline them? What don't you like about me?"

She held his face with both hands. "It's not you, it's both of us. I think we could work through this business of your wealth and my pride. But your urge to protect the women in your life—specifically your mother— would cause problems between us."

"What's my mother got to do with this?"

"More than you realize, I guess."

"Sarah, there's no way she could run the business, and I don't believe she'd want to try."

"Have you asked her?"

"I wouldn't consider it, not when she has so much on her mind."

"But you might give her something exciting to anticipate."

"Or one more thing to worry about. No, Sarah. Not now."

"How about...a rain check?"

"God, you're persistent."

"You said that's a quality one needs in the business world. I'm sure your mother has it, too."

"Ever think of selling real estate, Ms Melton?"

She grinned and shook her head. "Not interested. But I could if I wanted to."

"I'm beginning to believe it." He drew her into his arms. "Want to see which stores are open tonight?"

"Okay."

"Although if you'd rather do something else," he

continued, nuzzling her ear, "I could buy a dress without you."

"You don't know my size."

"That's what you think. I could pick out a perfect fit. I've been taking your measurements for days." His hand slid from the small of her back over the curve of her bottom. "Like this," he murmured, bringing her hips against his. "And this." His other hand cupped one breast and squeezed gently.

Sarah tilted her head back, and Cliff kissed his way down her throat to the V of her blouse. With one sensual touch he turned all her misgivings into wispy bits of nonsense. Reality became the heat radiating through her as he slowly unbuttoned her blouse and took one rosy nipple in his mouth. She moaned softly and arched upward shamelessly, wanting him to love her. Just one more time.

11

"YES, THAT WAS THE RIGHT DRESS." Cliff stood in the middle of Sarah's tiny living room while she twirled in front of him. "Right color, too. That sea green is beautiful with your hair. I'm a little afraid to take you to my mother's tonight, Sarah. Some liberated guy with less money and tougher trivia questions might snatch you away from me."

She smoothed the lapel of his cream-colored sport jacket. "I'm not looking for someone else, Cliff. Don't worry about that."

"Thanks." He gathered her into his arms, careful not to rumple her dress or disturb her hair. "Can I even kiss you, pretty woman?"

"If you don't mind lipstick on you," she whispered, winding her bare arms around his neck. His pale blue shirt was silk; the navy tie probably was, too. Damn him, he even smelled rich. But he was the man she loved.

"A gentleman always carries a handkerchief for postkissing purposes," Cliff murmured, dipping his head.

Sarah gave herself up to the sweetness of his kiss, allowing herself to believe, for this quiet moment, that all would be well.

With a moan of regret, Cliff relinquished her lips and reached in his back pocket for a monogrammed handkerchief. "This party will be rough," he said, wiping pink smudges from his mouth. "I'm used to having you to myself. How can I manage not being able to kiss you whenever I want to?"

"I'll be in the same boat, Cliff. It's only one evening."

"And the party means a lot to Mom. I hope Dad understands enough of what's going on to make all the preparations worthwhile."

"Even if he doesn't, you and your mother will know you did the best you could for him."

"Right. By the way, you'll have to put on more lipstick before we leave. I kissed it all away."

"In that case, how about one more for the road?"

"Sarah Jane, you're a wicked lady. And I love you for it." His second kiss was longer and more thorough, and by the time he was finished, they were both breathing hard.

"Put on your lipstick," he said, turning away, "or we'll never get out of here."

The warm scent of leather greeted Sarah a few minutes later as Cliff helped her into the car. Would she ever adjust to riding in a Mercedes?

As they glided away from the curb, Cliff took her hand. "Your fingers are cold. Nervous?"

"Maybe a little."

"They're just people, Sarah, with problems and triumphs like anyone else."

"I'll try to remember that."

They rode in silence through the shadowy foothills of the Catalinas. The moon highlighted the carved slopes of the mountains, which soon drew so close that Sarah felt as if she could reach out and touch them. At the entrance to an exclusive development, Cliff waved casually to the watchman at the gatehouse.

"Do your parents live on the golf course?"

"Mmm-hmm. But it's still just a house, Sarah. A place to eat and sleep."

"You could say that about Buckingham Palace."

"And I'd be right."

The house was everything Sarah had expected and hadn't seen in Cliff's own home. The two-story structure dominated the landscape, challenging the mountain backdrop with its elaborate pillars and grandiose, sweeping porch topped with red Spanish tile. The spotless windows reflected the sparkle of chandeliers and the polished glow of dark walnut furniture.

Cliff maneuvered the car between a Cadillac and a Lincoln Continental, then turned to Sarah. "Ready?"

"No."

"It'll be all right. I love you."

"I love you, too."

The noise from the house seemed to swell just then, as if the party were moving outside to engulf the two of them as they sat quietly in the moonlight. Sarah looked

at Cliff and tried to block out the voices bubbling from
the open windows of the house. It didn't work.

"Let's go in," she said with a sigh.

Cora Hamilton, clad in red georgette, materialized at
Sarah's elbow the moment she and Cliff stepped into
the cathedrallike living room. Cora greeted them
warmly, but her gaze quickly skittered from their faces
to dart around the room.

Sarah was reminded of a small bird poised for flight,
and she wondered how Cliff's mother felt living in a
house created for giants. Yet, as Sarah continued to ob-
serve Cora, she didn't seem particularly intimidated by
her large-scale surroundings. She gripped Sarah's arm
firmly and propelled her away from Cliff and into a
mélange of strange faces.

"You look lovely, Sarah," Cora said, guiding her
through the sleek, well-mannered gathering. In one
corner a string quartet performed, and waiters
threaded through the crowd offering drinks and hors
d'oeuvres.

"Where's Mr. Hamilton?" Sarah looked around for
Cliff's father.

"Over in that easy chair, surrounded by his old cro-
nies. So far, so good. He was making reasonable conversation the last time I checked. You were right to
urge me to do this, Sarah."

"I hope so."

"I'm sure of it. Ah, there are Jean and Henry. You
must meet them. Cliff's godparents. And of course I'll

introduce you to the Hildebrants. Cliff played with their boy from the time they were babies, and— Jean! I'd like you to meet Sarah Melton, Cliff's friend."

"Are you, by any chance, in real estate, too?" Jean inquired politely, fingering the large pearl at her earlobe.

"No, I work at TMC," Sarah replied, deciding to be vague.

"Really? I know one of the chief surgeons there, Mat Dobson. Perhaps you know him?"

"I know who he is, but we've never met," Sarah murmured. "It's a big hospital," she amended, feeling apologetic that she wasn't on speaking terms with a legend like Mat Dobson.

"Don't I know it," Cora moaned. "It takes an army of volunteers to keep the human touch in such a big institution. If you'll excuse us, Jean, I'm going to introduce Sarah to some of the other guests. Remind me to discuss a fund-raising matter with you later." Cora steered Sarah away. "You look petrified, dear. Don't let these people scare you."

"You sound like Cliff."

"Or Cliff sounds like me?"

Sarah chuckled. "That would make more sense."

"Sometimes I do make sense," Cora said with a little laugh and a return of her self-deprecating manner. And then her voice rose in greeting. "And how is the famous luck of the Hildebrants? Have you still got that stock-market bull by the horns?"

"We try to hold on to some part of his anatomy, anyway," commented a portly man in his fifties. "Who's the sweet young thing you have with you, Cora?"

"This is Sarah Melton, a good friend of Cliff's. Sarah, I'd like you to meet Graham and Mitsy Hildebrant. We've known them for years."

"Must you always say it like that, Cora?" complained Mitsy good-naturedly. "You make me feel ancient."

"I'll tell you what makes me feel ancient." Graham sipped his drink. "I can remember when our kids used to play in the back room during these parties, and now they're out here drinking hard liquor with the rest of us."

"Which reminds me," said Cora. "What will you have, Sarah?"

Sarah's mind raced. What did one order at a function like this? Champagne? "I—I'll have whatever you're having, Cora," she stammered.

Cliff's mother laughed. "Ginger ale?"

"Sure." Sarah felt a rush of warmth for the older woman. Anybody who wasn't afraid to drink ginger ale at her own posh party had Sarah's respect.

"I'll get us each a glass. I'm sure the Hildebrants will amuse you while I'm gone. By the way, folks, Sarah's an X-ray technician at TMC."

The smiling man and woman in front of Sarah nodded as if they'd been told Sarah were a brilliant young intern, and Sarah began to relax. Perhaps she could be herself among these people, after all.

"Have you known Cliff long, Sarah?" Mitsy asked.

"We went to high school together. Then we lost track of each other for several years, but when Cliff had his accident at Fort Lowell, I was on duty."

"And high school sweethearts were reunited! How romantic!" Mitsy exclaimed.

Sarah flushed. "Well, not exactly. In high school Cliff and I didn't—"

"That's right," Graham put in. "I remember Cliff was pretty involved with Alice and John's daughter, Julie. Remember, Mitsy?"

Mitsy sipped her drink reflectively. "I can't recall the whole thing. Didn't our Jim date Julie for a while? But I guess maybe— I don't know. Those kids all ran around together, but somehow I don't remember you, Sarah. Refresh my memory. Were you at Cliff's graduation party? Or maybe that thing we had after the prom...?"

"No, I—" Sarah's head began to throb.

"Here comes John now," Mitsy interrupted with a smile. "John? Please come over and answer a burning question."

"If you want to proposition me, Mitsy, you should have the good taste not to do it in front of your husband," joked a tall, lithe man who looked younger than his gray hair indicated he was.

Sarah flinched. This must be Julie DeWeese's father, and now all these terribly sophisticated people would discuss Cliff and Julie's dating days. And why shouldn't they? They'd all known each other and each other's children for years. She was the outsider here. Her headache grew worse.

"John, weren't Julie and Cliff an item in high school? We got on the subject because Sarah, here, ran around with our kids in high school, and we're trying to remember—"

"No, Mrs. Hildebrant, I didn't—" Sarah began, but she was cut off by John DeWeese.

"Julie and Cliff dated for a brief time in high school," he said smoothly. "Back then, Cliff was hell-bent on becoming a poverty-stricken history professor. Julie figured out that wasn't the sort of life she wanted. By the time Cliff woke up to the realities of life, Julie was taken."

Sarah bristled. "I understood Cliff left graduate school to help his father, not because he didn't want a history degree."

"Is that right?" John DeWeese's silver eyebrows rose. "You know him so well, then? What's your last name again? I can't seem to place you."

"I tried to say before that I didn't belong to Cliff's crowd in high school."

"I didn't think you looked familiar," DeWeese said coolly.

"John, Sarah came to the party with Cliff tonight," Mitsy said, glancing nervously at Sarah.

"That's nice," DeWeese said. "Cliff's a good catch,

now that he's given up his silly ideas of being a college professor."

"He hasn't—" Sarah faltered, wondering why she was explaining anything to this arrogant man.

"She and Cliff knew each other in high school, although I guess not well, and they've met again recently," Mitsy explained to fill the uncomfortable gap in the conversation.

"Ah. High school friends can lose track of each other, with everyone going away to school and all." His slate-colored eyes seemed to take in every detail about Sarah.

He's deciding I don't belong here, she concluded bitterly.

"Where did you go to school, Sarah?" He waited like a cat at a gopher hole, as if he knew what her answer would be. "Vassar? Bryn Mawr?"

"No." Sarah's fingers grew ice-cold, and the color drained from her face. "I couldn't afford to go *away* to school like the rest of your children." Her eyes swept the small group gathered around her. "My father's an unemployed copper miner from Catalina, and I struggled to get training through Pima College so I could hold some sort of decent-paying job. That's where I've been since high school. Now if you'll excuse me, I want to wish Mr. Hamilton a happy birthday."

Head high, she walked away from the group, shutting her ears to the murmured comments behind her. Let them think what they wanted. She'd never meet any of them again, anyway. This party showed her, in Technicolor detail, why a life with Cliff Hamilton was impossible.

Blinking back her tears, she approached the leather armchair where Jack Hamilton sat sipping from a tall glass.

"Happy birthday, Mr. Hamilton."

The older man looked up with a twinkle in his eye that reminded Sarah of Cliff. "I don't think it's really my birthday," he confided. "But everyone's having such a great time I hate to tell them. Are you one of Cliff's friends?"

Sarah hesitated. "Yes." A true friend would break off a relationship that could only bring heartbreak to both of them, she thought.

"I didn't catch your name."

"Sarah Melton."

"Well, Sarah, I need some advice about Cliff. I've been working him into the business a little at a time, but he doesn't seem to be taking to it. Has some idea of being a history professor, God knows why. Can't make any money at that."

Sarah blinked and tried to adjust herself to Jack Hamilton's garbled view of the world. "You're right. A college professor wouldn't make as much as you do with Hamilton Realty."

"Cliff's never lived without money. I don't think he realizes how strapped he'll feel, but I'm considering letting him do what he wants. What do you think, Sarah?''

She gazed down at the thin man in the leather chair. In spite of his confusion, he had some grasp of the situation.

"Not an easy question, is it?"

"No," she agreed, "it's not." She glanced around the room and spotted Cliff in a crowd of tanned, laughing people in their late twenties. He looked perfectly at ease, and very far away. Cora stopped by the group, a glass in each hand, and spoke to her son. He put his arm around her, the expression on his face tender and protective.

Watching them together, Sarah made her decision. Her presence, with her background and her ideas about Cora Hamilton's taking over the business, could only disrupt what was a workable, if not perfect, situation.

"I think Cliff belongs at Hamilton Realty," she said. "He can always teach a night course in history now and then."

"That's a good idea," Cliff's father said. "Splendid idea. Yes, Cliff needs to make good money. He's the type who enjoys living in style."

"Yes." Through a shimmer of tears, Sarah watched Cliff take a glass from his mother and work his way toward her. The best thing she could do for this man she loved was to leave him alone, allow him to continue his life as he'd been living it before she'd arrived on the scene. When he took her home tonight, their fantasy would come to an end.

SARAH'S RED-RIMMED EYES swept the lush spring growth around her. Last night's confrontation, the angry words, the uncomprehending look on Cliff's face, wouldn't leave her, despite the golden beauty of the paloverdes and the violet contrast of the ironwoods.

Even the thorny cactus plants were budding, preparing their once-a-year challenge to the desert. But for the first time in her life, her great-grandfather's land refused to heal her lacerated spirit. She should never have brought Cliff here because the very place that had once soothed her had become another reminder of his kisses, his soft words, his gentle touch.

Angrily she started the Volkswagen's motor and drove the rutted road back to the highway. As long as she was this far, she might as well visit her parents rather than waste the gas completely.

"Well, little bug," she said, patting the car's dashboard, "we're back on the road to where we came from, going back where we belong, girl."

Her parents' mobile home looked shabbier than she'd remembered it. One of her brothers must have kicked a football into the aluminum siding, and a section of the skirting was loose where Mittens and her brood had made an opening to crawl under the trailer. The lawn, or what struggled to become a lawn despite the onslaught of five active boys, needed a total replanting. She sighed and shut off the car engine. Was she unconsciously comparing the scene before her to the opulence of the Hamilton home?

She found her mother leaning over a large kettle of soup. "Don't they ever let you out of the kitchen, lady?" she asked, giving her mother a quick kiss on the cheek.

"Sarah! What a nice surprise." Ann Melton turned from the steaming kettle and smiled at her daughter, then took a closer look. "You've either got spring allergies, which you never had before, or something's wrong. Your eyes are a mess."

"Must be allergies," Sarah hedged halfheartedly. What she really wanted was to pour her heart out.

"Hmm. Two visits in such a short time is very flattering but highly unusual, Sarah. Would you by chance be having heart trouble?"

Sarah plopped into a seat at the kitchen table. How many times had she sat in this same chair and discussed her boyfriend problems with her mother? But they all seemed so small, so childish, compared to the ache that consumed her now.

Her mother poured two cups of coffee and placed one in front of Sarah before sitting down to sip her own. "Okay, what gives?"

"Do you remember Cliff Hamilton?"

Her mother looked startled. "Why, yes, as a matter of fact. Your father and I were just—"

"He turned up in the TMC emergency room not long

ago," Sarah said, rushing through the story before she lost her nerve. "A horse kicked him in the head. By the way, I'll probably be in a movie. Anyway, Cliff sailed into my life—and last night I pushed him out to sea."

"Cliff Hamilton is the reason for the red eyes?"

Sarah nodded.

"Oh. That puts a different light on things."

"A different light on what, Mom?"

"Never mind. Back up a minute. What did you say about a movie? I'm not sure I follow this."

Sarah laughed shortly. "Okay. Maybe I'd better start at the beginning." Briefly she outlined recent events, skimming over the obvious fact that she and Cliff had made love.

Predictably, her mother zeroed in on that very aspect. "If you're sexually involved with this man, then you don't have to tell me how much you value the relationship. Are you sure things couldn't be worked out?"

"I don't see how. Cliff has resisted asking his mother to become involved in the business, even though I know he's unhappy. But then, I don't know if Cliff could be content with a college professor's salary. He's used to so much more."

"If he's put time and effort into the business, I'd think his mother would insist he take a share of the profits, Sarah. He wouldn't have to live entirely on a teaching income."

Sarah glanced at her mother with a flicker of hope in

her brown eyes. "I hadn't thought of that." Then she shook her head. "He wouldn't take money from a business when he wasn't contributing, no matter what he'd accomplished in the past."

Her mother reached across the table and touched Sarah's hand. "Are you sure you can't accept the situation as it is?"

"Yes, I'm sure." She smiled forlornly. "I would always believe Cliff had shortchanged himself, and his mother. That's no way to make a marriage work."

Her mother held her coffee mug in both hands, resting her elbows on the table while she considered the situation. "Did you tell him all that?"

"No. Then he might feel blackmailed into changing everything just so I'd stay. That's not right, either."

"Still, Cliff has a right to—"

Eddie poked his head in the kitchen doorway. "Who's Cliff?"

"Just a friend of Sarah's. We're busy right now, Eddie."

"Well, geez! Dad's working on his computer books, Dave's on the phone to his girlfriend, Larry's up the street and Todd and Bill've got homework."

"Then come and talk to us," Sarah offered. She hadn't expected her mother to take Cliff's side—Eddie was a welcome distraction. "Who's going to win the pennant this year?"

"The Cubs are starting out awful good," Eddie said earnestly. "Who do you think?"

"You know me. I'm a Cardinal fan." Sarah settled in for a baseball discussion with her brother.

Ann Melton lifted one eyebrow, then rose to check the soup.

Mom couldn't know what dating someone like Cliff was like, Sarah thought as Eddie listed baseball statistics. This was one time when she didn't understand the problem.

DURING LUNCH SARAH LEARNED that the real-estate agent, Al Hollencraft, wasn't bringing out many prospects to look at the land. "When does the listing expire?" she asked.

"Not for another six weeks," her father answered. "But Al suggested we get somebody in Tucson. He knows how much we need the money."

"Have you got anyone in mind?"

"No," her mother said too quickly.

Sarah noticed the look that passed between her parents. "What about Hamilton Realty?"

Her father cleared his throat. "Your mother...told me briefly in the kitchen about your, ah, involvement with Cliff Hamilton, and I don't see any reason to—"

Sarah took a deep breath. "That's silly. If Hamilton Realty is the best company for the job, then that's who you should hire. I doubt if Cliff would handle our property himself, anyway, with the number of agents he has."

"Sarah," her mother put in softly, her expression

troubled, "I don't know quite how to phrase this, but is there a chance, after you two parted with angry words..." She fidgeted with her napkin, then plunged on. "Is there any chance he wouldn't want to list our property? We're the only Meltons in Catalina, so he's bound to know who we are."

"Oh, I'm sure he wouldn't—" Sarah began.

"Are you?" her mother interjected.

Sarah studied the ice cubes slowly diluting her tea while she considered her mother's words. Cliff had been very upset last night. How *would* he react to dealing with her parents? Surely his professionalism would assert itself, and yet...

She raised her eyes and looked from one concerned face to the other. Her actions might very well make the difference between a rosy future and a dismal one for these two people she loved.

And then, slowly, a plan began to take shape in her mind. Perhaps her precious land wouldn't be lost, after all.

"I'll go see Cliff myself," Sarah said.

"We can't ask you to do that." Her father shifted uneasily in his chair.

"You didn't. I offered. I'll see Cliff and ask him if our personal problems would prevent him from listing your property. If he gives me any reason to believe he won't do a professional job, then we'll have to try someone else. I can't imagine that will happen, but after I've talked with Cliff, I'll be sure. I can go tomorrow morning after work." Sarah glanced at her mother, who had a strange little smile on her face. "Okay, Mom?"

"I think you're right to go," Ann Melton said, and her eyes sparkled as if she were privy to a wonderful joke. "Let her do it, David."

"I hate to," her father said gruffly, then glanced at his wife and saw the expression on her face. "Don't I?"

"No," said Ann, catching her lower lip between her teeth and shaking her head.

"Now, Mom," Sarah cautioned brusquely, "I can see the wheels turning. This is business, nothing more."

"Certainly!" her mother said, her eyes round with innocence. "I never said it wasn't."

Sarah cast a censuring look in her mother's direction. What a romantic she was. Just because Sarah would be seeing Cliff again, her mother thought something might come of the meeting. Nothing would, of course. She had meant it when she said she and Cliff were through. Why, then, was her stomach doing flip-flops at the thought of tomorrow's mission?

12

SARAH SUBMERGED HERSELF in a sea of work at the hospital that night. When her tasks dwindled at about three o'clock in the morning, she gave the lab a thorough cleaning. Perhaps exhaustion, she reasoned, would still the jangling of her nerves whenever she thought of confronting Cliff again so soon.

Yet by the time she drove home to change her clothes, her body felt as tightly strung as her father's hunting bow. Two hours stretched ahead of her before she could call Cliff's office to make an appointment. She could contact him earlier at home, but Sarah wanted to work through his secretary to eliminate any personal overtones.

Nothing in her closet suited the impression she wanted to convey. Who was she trying to kid? Sarah Melton didn't own the kind of outfit she needed for this interview. If a fairy godmother had suddenly appeared, Sarah would have ordered up a white linen suit and spectator pumps. Maybe even a nifty little hat with a brim that half-concealed her face. She wanted to look like Meryl Streep or Faye Dunaway.

Furiously she worked on the black marks marring her white shoes, a pair of sandals with modest two-inch heels. Her only spring dress, a simple cotton wraparound, was pink. Hadn't someone told her no one takes a woman dressed in pink seriously? She sighed and put on the dress. Couldn't be helped.

She paced back and forth across her tiny living room as the kitchen clock's hands dragged toward nine. The telephone book lay open on a chair, in case the number she knew by heart flew from her memory halfway through the dialing process. At last she picked up the receiver with a trembling hand.

Cliff's secretary sounded efficient and well paid. "I'll check with Mr. Hamilton and see what his schedule is this morning, Miss Melton," she said in a modulated voice. "Would you hold, please?"

"Yes." Sarah dropped to the chair and crossed her legs to stop them from shaking. Her palms began to sweat, and she cradled the receiver against her shoulder and wiped her hand on the chair's upholstered arm.

"Mr. Hamilton can see you at nine-thirty," came the crisp voice. "But he asked me to tell you he has a meeting at ten. Will you be able to conclude your business in that length of time?"

"Yes," Sarah said again. "Thank you." She consulted the kitchen clock again and calculated she'd just make it. "I'll be there in twenty-five minutes."

Her Volkswagen, however, had other ideas. Frantically Sarah turned the key and pumped the pedal until a strong odor of gas convinced her she'd flooded the engine.

"Little bug, how can you do this to me?" she wailed, collapsing back in the seat. She felt her cotton dress crinkling under her.

The weather report promised temperatures above normal for early May, and the interior of the car was already quite warm. Sarah rolled down the window and waited for the excess gas to drain from the carburetor. No doubt about it—she would be late.

At fifteen minutes past nine, the car reluctantly chugged to life. Sarah wiped the drops of perspiration from her upper lip, prayed her deodorant would hold up for the next forty-five minutes and pulled into traffic.

She made good time until she hit a construction zone. A gigantic yellow earthmover lumbered across the road and sent a layer of dust through her open window.

The flagwoman waved the opposite line of cars through the one-way detour first, and Sarah added another five minutes to her already late arrival time. She smiled grimly as a Cadillac and a Lincoln passed, each with windows rolled up and air conditioners wafting cool breezes over the well-dressed occupants.

By the time Sarah turned into the parking lot of Cliff's office building, it had to be nearly nine forty-five. She was sweaty, dusty and late. The contrast between the impression she had longed to make and the one she would make almost brought her to tears. But this visit was necessary if she wanted to help her parents, and if Cliff agreed to cooperate, the land might be saved.

Sarah straightened her shoulders and marched into the air-conditioned lobby of Hamilton Realty. "Sarah Melton to see Mr. Hamilton," she told the secretary.

The secretary frowned at her watch and reached for the intercom button. "Sarah Melton has arrived, Mr. Hamilton. Are you still available?"

"Send her in, please, Miss Dickson."

The sound of Cliff's voice coming from the brown box made Sarah want to run out of the carpeted lobby, away from the glossy potted plants, from a world where a well-turned-out Miss Dickson sat behind a tidy desk and silently censured Sarah's tardiness.

"Right through that door," said the unsmiling Miss Dickson with a wave of her hand.

Sarah hesitated. Couldn't another company handle her parents' property just as well? She knew the answer. Hamilton had the best advertising, the largest staff, a network of contacts across the country.

Besides, just any company might not help her with the plan she'd formulated yesterday. Cliff might not, either, but he was her only chance. For the next fifteen minutes she had to be strong. She could stand anything for fifteen minutes. Quickly she strode to the dark-paneled door and turned the knob.

As he heard the door open, Cliff bent his head over the stack of papers in front of him. He scribbled something across the top of one, hoping he hadn't just marked up an important deed of trust because he had no idea what he'd written. Her footsteps were muted as she walked across the thick carpet to his desk.

"Cliff?"

"Yes?" He looked up as if relinquishing an engrossing task. "Why, Sarah, how nice to see you."

"I'm sorry I'm late."

"Are you late?" He shoved back the sleeve of his sport coat and consulted his watch. "I guess you are. I was so busy with paperwork I lost track of time."

He found himself gobbling her up with hungry eyes, and he glanced out the window before she could notice. For the past fifteen minutes he'd been prowling the confines of his office as he prayed that nothing had happened to her. And why was she late, damn it? Didn't she think enough of him to be on time?

"My car wouldn't start." She adjusted the shoulder strap of her white purse. "And I forgot about the construction zone, so—"

"Don't worry about it," Cliff said magnanimously. She looked marvelous—all rumpled and warm and moist from the heat. He could easily imagine her in the throes of passion when she looked like that. Most of the women he came into contact with during business hours clung to air-conditioned rooms and cars as if heat and sweat were terminal. "Why don't you sit down?"

"Thank you." Sarah perched on the edge of one of the leather office chairs arranged in front of Cliff's desk. "My business won't take long, and you can get on to your meeting."

Cliff saw no reason to tell her that when she'd failed to arrive on time, he'd canceled his ten o'clock meeting. Until she showed her hand, he'd play his very close to his vest. "And what is your business, Sarah?" He allowed only the mildest curiosity to slip into his question. Maybe he'd become a movie actor yet.

"My parents' land," she replied, folding and unfolding the strap of her purse where it lay in her lap.

"Oh?" Cliff cursed silently. She really was here on business! During the interminable hours since they'd parted, he'd longed for some sign that she'd reconsidered, that she wanted to reestablish contact, and when she'd called the office that morning, he'd let himself hope....

He rose from the chair and came from behind the desk to sit in the chair opposite hers. If this was a business call, he'd have to work to squeeze the most out of it, and he'd begin by putting her in full view.

How he cherished those long, sleek legs, the generous breasts under the pink cotton dress, the— He restrained his fevered memories as they began taking their toll on his body. After all, he was in full view of her, too.

"Al Hollencraft isn't getting much action on the property." She kept her eyes averted. "He's agreed to release my folks from the listing agreement, and your company is the next obvious choice."

Hope leaped again in Cliff's heart. Maybe this had possibilities, after all. "I see no problem with that."

"I was sure you wouldn't," Sarah said in a rush.

"But my parents were afraid—that is, they know we've dated, and..."

Dated? Cliff wanted to shake her right out of her prim little perch on the chair. *We made wild, wonderful love together!* he wanted to shout. *And that's about as close to dating as a tea party is to an orgy.* "What does our—" he cleared his throat "—*dating* have to do with your parents' property?"

"They thought that under the circumstances you might not want to list it. I told them you were a professional, and besides, one of your employees would handle the whole thing, anyway. Still, I decided to discuss the matter with you so I could set their fears to rest."

Cliff's gaze was riveted on her creamy throat as she swallowed nervously. Could he sit so close to her and not put his lips against that vulnerable hollow above her collarbone?

"You were right, of course, Sarah. I wouldn't let any personal, ah, matters interfere with placing all the resources of my business at your parents' disposal."

"Thank you. That's the first part of my business. There's something else."

"God, I hope so."

She glanced up, startled. "No, not what you're thinking, Cliff."

"Sarah—"

"Please, don't make this more difficult."

"I can't imagine how it could be more difficult."

"Then let's drop the whole thing." She rose from her chair. "I shouldn't have made the appointment."

"Wait," he said quietly. "Forget what I said. What else did you want to discuss?"

She studied him for a moment, then slowly sat down again. "I want to buy the property, secretly of course, so my parents won't know. Could you arrange that?"

"You can't afford to buy it."

She stiffened. "That's none of your business. Can you arrange an anonymous sale or not?"

"It can be done. The land can be bought by a trust, which would be you. My lawyer can arrange it for you."

"I'll pay whatever extra fee is necessary."

"No fee." His face was impassive.

"Cliff, lawyers always charge something."

He struck the arms of his chair with the flat of each hand. "Damn it, Sarah! All right. I'll add his fee to the closing costs. You are the stubbornest, proudest—" *Most desirable woman in the world. I want you so much I can't see straight.*

"I want this to be on the level, that's all."

"I hate to think what you're sacrificing to pay for this. What will you do, work two jobs?"

"No. I have enough in my college account for the down payment, and the rest can be financed."

"You'd have to tell them sometime."

"I will, after Dad's making a decent living. They'll want to pay me back, so I'll wait until I know they can."

"I take it you've already offered your college savings and they won't take them."

"That's right."

Cliff shook his head. "Of course. You had to get that stubborn pride from somewhere. Okay, Sarah Jane. You've got a deal."

"Good." She stood up again.

He pushed himself from his chair, suddenly bringing them just inches from each other. He could see the tired little shadows under her eyes, and his arms ached from holding them at his sides. "My secretary will draw up the necessary papers, and I'll take them out to your parents' place tomorrow."

"You?"

Her eyes widened, and her lips parted in surprise. If he kissed her now, she wouldn't be able to close her mouth quickly enough to keep him from plunging his tongue deep inside her, from tasting— He closed his eyes briefly and clenched his hands.

"I don't delegate all the business to my employees, Sarah."

"I know, but surely in this case—"

"Especially in this case." He had to act fast, or she'd slip through his fingers. She needed something from him. That something wasn't what he'd hoped, but he would work with what weapons she'd provided.

"I don't understand," she said faintly.

"All this secrecy business. I can't turn something like that over to another agent and risk having a slipup."

"I guess you're right."

"But I have a condition."

"A condition?"

He watched her lips form the words. She'd eaten off nearly all her lipstick; only a slight pink line surrounded the full pout of her mouth. One good kiss and even that would be gone. "When I come out to list the property, I want you to be there. I want you to be my personal guide during the inspection tour."

"But why? You've seen most of it already. You know where it is, what it looks like."

"Very simple. You need something from me, and I believe it's only fair for me to get something I want out of this. What I want is time alone with you." He flinched at the helpless despair in her eyes.

"Cliff, what we had is over. Let it die."

"Not a chance."

"You'll only make us both more miserable."

"Sarah, I couldn't be more miserable. Will you agree to my terms or not?"

"I guess nobody gets a free lunch, huh?" she muttered through clenched teeth.

"No, Sarah, nobody does. I'll be at your parents' place at about two o'clock tomorrow, if that's convenient."

"Better make it one. My mother takes her break from the grocery store then."

"Oh. Sorry. I didn't realize she had a job outside the home."

"I'm sure you didn't," she snapped with a tilt of her chin. "Mothers don't work, do they?"

He gave her a piercing look. "That's what this is all

about, isn't it? My attitude toward my mother taking over the business."

"I'd rather not discuss it."

"We'll see about that, Sarah. Will you tell your parents when to expect me?"

"Yes." Her brown eyes flashed in rebellion.

"And you, Sarah? Will you be expecting me?"

"I'll be there," she said tightly.

"Leave their address with Miss Dickson on your way out," Cliff directed, then moved away from her and back around his desk with a supreme effort. He'd won a small reprieve from their enforced separation, and he didn't want to blow it. "If you'll excuse me, I have a ten o'clock meeting."

Without another word she turned and stalked from the office, and his resolve to stay aloof nearly melted at the furious twitch of her behind as she stepped through the door. If he ran after her, he could catch her before she reached Dickson's desk, and— No. Tomorrow. Tomorrow was better.

"Okay, let me get this straight." Sarah's father paced the worn carpet in his living room. "After we sign the listing papers, Cliff Hamilton wants you, not your mother or me, to show him the property?"

"That's his condition, Dad."

"Can this man be trusted with our daughter, Ann?"

Sarah's mother hid a smile. "I'm sure he can, David. I remember Cliff Hamilton as a very nice boy in high school. He's a college graduate and a successful businessman, and even though I suspect he has a rather large crush on Sarah, I think he can be trusted."

"Mom!" Sarah turned a horrified gaze on her mother.

"It's quite obvious he wants to talk with you alone, Sarah," her mother insisted. "You can show him the property as well as either of us, and I think you ought to hear him out, anyway. If he wants to use this opportunity to get you to listen, I have to give him credit for being an enterprising suitor."

"Suitor! Now just a minute, I—"

"I suggest we hold the noise down," her father cautioned. "Someone just drove up." He parted the curtain and looked out the window. "Must not be him, though. It's an old pickup truck."

Sarah stood up from her chair. "Tan? About twenty years old?"

"Uh-huh."

"That's him."

Her father looked over his shoulder in confusion. "I thought one of your objections to this man was that he was too high-toned?"

"Don't let the truck fool you, Dad. He also owns a Mercedes."

"Oh." Her father dropped the curtain and walked to the door. "Still, a man who drives a good old pickup like that can't be all bad, Sarah."

Sarah heard Cliff's step on the porch and adjusted her belt. Her name was stamped across the back in inch-high letters.

"You must be Cliff Hamilton," her father said as he opened the door before Cliff could knock. "Come on in. I'm David Melton, Sarah's father."

"Glad to meet you." Cliff took off his straw cowboy hat and shook her father's hand. "I understand you're into computers these days."

Sarah's father nodded. "I hope an old dog can learn new tricks. The copper industry isn't a dependable source of income for me anymore."

"If you're anything like your daughter, I imagine you can do whatever you set your mind to, Mr. Melton." He glanced at Sarah, but she refused to meet his gaze.

"I hope you're right. I'd like you to meet my wife, Ann. Couldn't be doing any of this without her support. It was her idea to sell some of her grandfather's land to pay my tuition."

"And Grandpa would have approved," Ann Melton added. "He believed in looking toward the future, not the past. We have to adjust to the times, don't you agree, Cliff?"

"I guess you're right, Mrs. Melton." Cliff reached for the woman's outstretched hand. Judging by her assessing glance, he knew Sarah had been talking about him, about their relationship. Ann Melton was sizing him up, deciding whether to encourage his courtship of her daughter. That remark about adjusting to the times could have come from Sarah.

He reached into his pocket and pulled out a folded document. "Here's the listing agreement, Mr. Melton, if you'd like to look it over. Al Hollencraft supplied me with the property description."

Sarah's father put on his reading glasses and unfolded the papers. "Poor Al. Hated to take this away from him, but he wasn't getting very fast action."

"Maybe he's too nice a guy. I've tried to explain to Sarah what an aggressive business this is."

"Yeah, Dad. Have Cliff show you his thumbscrews and brass knuckles."

David Melton glanced at his daughter over the rim of his glasses. "That sounded sarcastic, young lady. I understand what Cliff means about Al. He's not a go-getter. I can see that Cliff is."

"So can I," Ann said with a muted chuckle.

Sarah glared at her. Whose side was her mother on, anyway?

"The listing looks fine to me." Sarah's father handed the papers to his wife. "You study it, Ann. You're the financial wizard in this family."

"Take your time," Cliff said. "Sarah promised me a tour of the property so I can talk about it more easily with clients. I'll pick up the agreement when I bring her back."

Sarah's father nodded. "Sounds good. Better take a jug of water. It's getting hot out there."

"I have one in the truck. Shall we go, Sarah?"

Silently she preceded him out the door. He opened the passenger's side of the truck, and before she could climb in, he boosted her up to the seat as he had the first time they'd ridden together. "Nice belt, Sarah."

He held her a moment longer than was necessary, and she began to shake. "Thank you."

"You can't deny your feelings, you know."

"Let's go, Cliff."

"All right." He dropped his gaze and closed the truck door.

By the time he rounded the truck and swung up beside her, she had made a decision. "Cliff, this isn't going to work."

He started the truck. "Sure it is."

"I thought I could deal with you on this land business, but I'm not that strong. Can you take me home? We'll make up some story that you forgot about another appointment. You don't have to look at the property at all if I'll be the buyer."

"You agreed to this, Sarah."

"I didn't realize—"

"That you can't turn love off that easily? I thought you were smarter than that, Marvelous Melton."

Her parents' trailer disappeared from sight as they turned onto the highway. She was alone with Cliff Hamilton—a precarious situation, indeed. "I'm not very smart," she said, nervously aware of his presence next to her. "I'm dumb, in fact. Dumb to ever imagine we could bridge the gaps between us."

"What damn gaps? You keep referring to these gaps, but when I ask you to be specific, you won't. Is it the money?"

"Not exactly. In a way, but..."

"Is it because I won't ask my mother to take over the

business so I can play college professor?" Cliff turned off the highway onto the dirt road leading to the property. They bounced along in silence. "Well, I guess that's it. Why won't you say so?"

"That's only part of the problem, Cliff," she said at last when he parked under the giant paloverde. "I'm afraid the way you treat your mother is the way you'd treat me. I don't want you to sacrifice your own happiness for me, put me on a pedestal."

He faced her, his blue eyes intense. "My happiness is you, Sarah."

"No," she whispered. "No, I don't think so."

"You're making this all so difficult. Why couldn't I buy this property from your parents? Why couldn't we get married and build a house on it? I don't understand what's wrong with that program, Sarah."

"I'd feel like a leech, that's what wrong with it. I'd be contributing to the end of your dream, just as your mother is, without knowing it."

"But I love you both!"

She wanted so much to touch him, but she kept her hands clenched in her lap. "I know, but that kind of love could smother me, Cliff."

"All right. Suppose I get my mother into the business. Would that make you happy?"

"No, because you'd be reorganizing everything for me, not for yourself and for her. You don't really believe it's the right decision, and you've got to be behind the change a hundred percent for it to work. I can't be the reason for it."

Cliff hit the steering wheel with his fist. "Damn it, Sarah. You don't leave us any room, do you?"

"That's because we don't belong together. I understand that now. I don't want to rock the boat. You should continue to run Hamilton Realty, and your mother should continue her charity work."

"Where do you fit into this little picture?"

"That's just it, Cliff. I don't."

"The hell you don't." In one swift movement he pulled her into his arms and brought his lips down on hers.

She squirmed in his firm grip, trying to wrench away from his kiss, but he held her fast. Her heart hammered against her ribs as he forced his tongue into her mouth and demanded her response. At her moan of desire, he fumbled with the buttons of her blouse.

"No, Cliff," she cried as his lips left hers and moved to her throat.

"You won't listen to logic," he said hoarsely against her skin. "I may not have your mind, but I sure as hell have your body." He unsnapped her bra and cupped one breast. "You can't deny what happens when I touch you like this."

"No, I can't." She was panting now. "But don't do this, Cliff. Don't try to use sex to change my mind."

Suddenly he was quiet. Then slowly he refastened her bra and buttoned her blouse. "You're right," he murmured, brushing back her hair and looking into her flushed face. "If our love isn't strong enough to change your mind, I don't want what your body offers, no matter how sweet. You win, Sarah Jane."

13

THE STRICKEN LOOK on Cliff's face as he turned away from her and started the truck burned itself into Sarah's brain. In the long days and nights that followed that afternoon, the agony in his blue eyes haunted her, no matter how often she told herself their separation was for the best. But why did it have to hurt so much?

The property sale was accomplished through intermediaries, and Sarah didn't see Cliff during the transaction. He didn't try to make personal contact, but after their last encounter, Sarah wasn't surprised.

Her parents were overjoyed with the land sale, and Sarah managed to change the subject whenever they brought up the mysterious buyer they'd never met.

One Sunday afternoon Sarah's mother hesitantly asked about Cliff, but Sarah explained that she and Cliff were permanently estranged. His name was not mentioned again, but Sarah could feel her mother's concern.

Outwardly Sarah's life returned to its routine. She worked her normal shifts and drove out to Catalina regularly to watch Eddie play baseball. She took comfort in his enthusiasm, his delight in catching balls with a new glove and running the bases in sparkling white cleats.

One day when she had an extra hour before Eddie's game started, Sarah took the dirt road to her favorite spot, expecting a feeling of elation that the land didn't belong to some stranger. Instead, she felt only emptiness and pain as memories of Cliff crowded around her.

She leaned against the steering wheel and fought tears of loneliness while his words echoed in her mind. "Why can't we get married and build a house here?" She relived the special moments they'd shared—the warmth of a campfire, country songs on the radio, bouts of history trivia and the passion. Would she ever forget their glorious lovemaking?

She put the car in gear and drove back to the highway. Maybe someday she would be able to enjoy the serenity of her great-grandfather's homestead again. But for now the magic of her special place was gone.

Summer arrived with a vengeance, and in July the summer monsoon added humidity to the furnace-hot air. Sarah's trips to her parents' trailer became increasingly uncomfortable without air-conditioning in her car, but she enjoyed watching her father's progress. His training was nearly finished, and he was considering several job offers. The boys had been promised an aboveground swimming pool after his first paycheck.

During her trips to Catalina Sarah usually tried to ignore the Hamilton Realty signs she passed on her way out of town. Reading Cliff's name didn't help her state of mind. But in spite of her resolve, a new bit of frontage that had been scraped clean of desert growth caught her eye. Commercial building along the road was inevitable, but she hated to see it, anyway. Probably another Hamilton Realty project.

She confirmed her suspicion when the Hamilton Realty logo became visible on the sign advertising the development. But the name beneath the logo caused her to swerve to the side of the road and look again. It was Hamilton, all right. Cora Hamilton.

CLIFF STOOD IN THE DOORWAY to his mother's office and watched her work. Sarah had been right. Cora had leaned on him because he'd allowed her to. When he consciously encouraged her to make her own decisions, she leaned less and less.

She'd absorbed information about the business like a sponge, but he had really pulled back to keep her from consulting him on every deal. Finally she began applying the skills she'd developed through her charity work, and now she was threatening to outsell some of his veterans.

Cliff longed to tell Sarah about it, but he couldn't call her. She'd misinterpret, think he was grandstanding for her benefit. He'd thought about how long he dared wait before contacting her. Long enough so that she'd know he was serious about bringing his mother into the business. Two months wasn't enough time.

But what if she found someone else while he waited?

Well, then, he'd have to set that guy straight. He wouldn't lose her without a fight.

"Mom, how's the sale of that office complex going?"

Cora raised her head and smiled. "Fine. But I'd feel better if you sat in on the bargaining session."

"You know enough to handle it."

"Cliff, this is a very big deal."

"And you're a very good agent. Besides, I have another appointment that morning."

"That you scheduled on purpose," she accused.

"Maybe. Just remember how proud you've been every time you've made a deal without me hanging around."

"Proud and scared to death."

"Less each time, I bet."

"I guess so. Sometimes I even have fun." Her eyes sparkled.

"Fun?"

"Sure. Don't you think the negotiating is fun?"

"Can't say I do, Mom."

Cora rested her chin in her hands and studied her son. "Cliff, sit down a minute."

He lowered himself to the chair in front of her desk.

"I always knew you weren't crazy about real estate, but I thought you liked the things it could buy, so I've kept my mouth shut."

"I do like the things it can buy."

"But you shouldn't spend your working life in a job that isn't fun for you. Life's too short."

He laughed. "The wisdom of the newly converted."

"Yes, but I mean it."

"Mom, for what I'd really like to do, I'd have to go back to school."

"So go back, at least part-time. Eventually, who knows?" She shrugged. "Maybe I'll take this entire operation off your hands."

"Think so?" He grinned. "Sounds tempting. But I can't afford to leave Hamilton Realty just yet."

"Why not?"

"Too drastic. A student doesn't make any money, and I need an income."

"You'd have an income. You know you can have a permanent income from the business."

"And you know I wouldn't take it."

"Cliff, sometimes you are so much like your father I don't know whether to strangle you or hug you. But I wish you'd take the money."

"I'm trying hard to be flexible these days, but drawing money from a business I wasn't helping operate would be more than my pride could handle. Sorry. Besides, I'd need more than you think."

"Oh?"

"If my plans work out, I'll be supporting two instead of one."

Cora sat up straight in her chair. "Another serious girlfriend, Cliff? Anybody I know?"

"Not another one, Mom. The same one. I hope Sarah will agree to marry me."

"I don't understand," Cora said with a frown. "I thought you and Sarah split up."

"We did. And at first I was so hurt and angry I told myself to forget her, go back to school and worry about finding a wife later."

"And?"

"And I can't forget her."

Cora's eyes filled with sympathy. "What are you going to do?"

"See her again, somehow."

"You don't have to discuss this, Cliff, but I wonder what has changed that makes you believe things will work out this time. I'd hate you to get hurt even worse."

"There are some changes. But I'm not sure the time's right to contact Sarah. You see, we had a big fight about the fact that I hadn't asked you to help with the business. She thought it was a good idea. At the time I resisted, but after we put Dad in the intermediate care facility, you were so lost...."

"And Sarah's idea made more sense to you." Cora's eyes widened. "You mean I have Sarah to thank for my new lease on life?"

"She planted the seed, but you've made it grow, Mom. I'm proud of you."

"Still, I'd like to thank that girl. Can't you call her, now that things are different? And if you can't, maybe I will."

"I wish you'd wait. If I run to her immediately and brag about what you and I have done, she'll think I arranged it to get her back, more as a token gesture than because I really understand what she meant."

"I could testify on your behalf. I don't feel the least mollycoddled anymore. Quite the contrary." Cora laughed. "Apparently we both needed Sarah to introduce us to the twentieth century."

"I just need her, period. But I have to be careful how I approach the situation."

"Okay, Cliff. I'll leave that to your discretion. But as soon as possible I'd like to talk to Sarah, thank her for a brilliant idea." She crossed her arms on the desk. "Now about this other matter. You don't want to give up your income so you'll have something to offer Sarah. But couldn't you take at least one course?"

"I'll think about it. I don't need the stimulation right now, anyway. Laramour's coming back to reshoot a sequence of the film this weekend, and Pat's asked me to another encampment."

"Watch out for flying horses' hooves, son."

"Hey, that's an idea. If I got kicked again, somebody would have to take me to the emergency room, and Sarah would be there to X-ray me, and—"

"Don't even think about it, Cliff."

"Just kidding, Mom. No, the perfect thing would be if Sarah would contact me. But I don't know if I'll be that lucky."

"HI, DAN. What's new?" Sarah wheeled the X-ray machine down the hall as the paramedic fell into step beside her.

"Not much. Say, remember that crazy crowd that

was filming some movie over at Fort Lowell last spring?"

"Mmm-hmm." Did she ever.

"On the way in this morning, I noticed they're back at it again."

"That's interesting." Her pulse quickened.

"Did you keep in touch with that guy, the one you knew from high school?"

"No."

"I wonder when that movie's coming out. I'd like to see it, wouldn't you?"

"Oh, not especially, Dan."

"Okay. I take the hint. Catch you later, Sarah."

"Sorry, Dan," she called after him. "I'm just antisocial, I guess." What was wrong with her? Dan was nice enough, and he'd been trying for weeks to ask her out. He'd gotten so desperate he was dropping hints about seeing a movie that wasn't even released yet.

Sarah parked the X-ray machine in its accustomed spot and walked down the hall to finish some paperwork before her shift was over. So Martin Laramour was back, along with F Troop. Was Cliff with them?

Several weeks had passed since she'd noticed Cora Hamilton's name on a Hamilton Realty sign. Weeks of not hearing from Cliff. Once she'd seen the sign, Sarah had expected him to call announcing that he'd taken her suggestion and now they could pick up where they'd left off. She was prepared to tell him they both needed more time.

But the call hadn't come, and Sarah was confused.

More than that, she was anxious to find out what was going on in Cliff's head. Perhaps Pat or Maureen would tell her. Cliff probably wasn't at the encampment, anyway. And if he was, so what? She could be a spectator just like anyone else.

Her decision to go to the park was made almost before she realized it. Minutes after her shift was over, she was sitting in her Volkswagen a little distance away from the encampment. No need to advertise her presence. She got out of the car and walked cautiously toward the row of tents.

She recognized several of the women from the first encampment; they were gathered around the fire circle. All the men were mounted and practicing charges in the open field. From this distance Sarah couldn't tell whether Cliff was among the soldiers cantering across the grass, but a tan pickup was parked next to Pat and Maureen's camper.

The familiar scene, complete with the film crew barking orders, brought an ache to her heart. How she and Cliff had fought that first day, and how they had loved the next morning!

The row of khaki tents reminded her of their torrid encounter just before dawn when she had first learned what it meant to be loved by Cliff Hamilton. And, God help her, she would always remember the magic of his touch, the fire of his kiss.

"Sarah! Sarah Melton!" Maureen's dark hair bounced against her shoulders as she ran forward. "Does Cliff know you're here?"

"No, I..."

Maureen's eyes narrowed. "Would you rather he didn't know?"

"In a way. I heard you were all over here, and I stopped to say hello, that's all."

"Why not stay?"

Sarah glanced over at the field. "How long will they be out there?"

"Another fifteen minutes, at least. Then there won't be another cavalry scene until this afternoon. Coffee?"

"Maybe just one cup, until they come back. I really don't want to see Cliff. I just wanted—"

"To know how he is? Terrible." Maureen handed her a tin cup of steaming coffee. "He and Pat stayed up last night drinking some of Pat's famous beer, and from what Pat said, Cliff is miserable without you, Sarah. Won't you talk with him?"

"He can't be very unhappy, Maureen. He hasn't called me. Why wouldn't he at least do that, if he wants to patch things up?"

"I can't answer that one."

"In fact, I've been expecting his call after..." She left the sentence unfinished.

"After what? This whole thing has me going. First, I thought you were both headed for the altar, and then poof, Cliff tells us he never wants to see you again."

"He said that?"

"Yes, but don't believe him. That was right after you two broke up, and he was a mess. Pat said last night he sounded different."

"Last night he was drunk."

"Let's say a little tipsy. Pat thinks he was sincere."

"Maybe and maybe not. I don't feel like taking the chance."

"Sarah, I can't keep this visit of yours a secret from him. That wouldn't be right."

"Okay, then don't say anything this weekend, but next time you see him, you can mention you ran into me and I asked about him. How about that? Then he can do whatever he wants with that information."

"I'm not wild about the idea, but if you insist."

"I do." Sarah drained her cup. "Thanks for the coffee and the conversation. I'd better get going before they come back."

"I think you're making a mistake, and Cliff will probably kill me if he ever finds out, but you're the boss. Goodbye, Sarah. Nice seeing you again."

"Goodbye, Maureen. And thanks."

Sarah turned and walked back through the cottonwoods. Why had she parked so far away, she thought, walking faster. Cliff never wanted to see her again? Of course he'd been hurt and angry, but to hear his words, even secondhand, filled her with anguish. She couldn't bear to have him say such a thing to her face.

She felt, rather than heard, the hoofbeats behind her, and before she could whirl around, strong arms pulled her into the air and flung her up on the tall horse's saddle.

"And where the hell did you think you were going?"

Sarah twisted and looked into flashing blue eyes

shaded by the bill of a Union soldier's cap. She smiled weakly. "Who was vice president under Herbert Hoover?"

"Charles Curtis. How could you show up here and then try to sneak away?"

"Ah-ha. But do you know who ran against Franklin Pierce in 1852?"

"No, and I don't care."

"Don't care? What kind of talk is that?"

"Shut up, Marvelous Melton." He kissed her soundly and thoroughly, leaving her gasping for breath. "Now will you tell me what this is all about or not?"

She clung to him, inhaling the smell of wool and leather. His horse snorted and pawed the grass impatiently. "Aren't you hot in this uniform?"

"Is that a leading question?"

"No! I just—"

"As a matter of fact, this jacket is very warm. Let's take a little ride to your apartment where I can slip into something more comfortable."

"To my apartment? That's four blocks away! You can't ride a horse to my apartment, especially dressed like that. People will think you're crazy."

"I don't care." He clucked to the horse, and they started across the park in the direction of Sarah's apartment.

"Cliff, put me down this minute. I'll tell you whatever you want to know, but let's not make a spectacle of ourselves. I don't exactly have a hitching post in my front yard. Where will we put this horse? I'll be evicted."

"I don't care."

"You don't care, you don't care. Is that all you can say?"

"Not by a long shot. But you've got some explaining to do first. Why did you come to the park this morning?"

"I, um, was curious about how you... That is, I—I saw your mother's name on a Hamilton Realty sign, Cliff." The horse's hooves clopped steadily along the quiet street.

"Oh, really? How long ago?"

"Three weeks. Naturally I wondered about it."

"You must not have wondered about it much, if it took three weeks before you thought to contact me."

"I expected you might contact me."

"And risk having you accuse me of engineering the whole thing for your benefit? Fat chance. And by the way, Franklin Pierce's opponent in the 1852 election was Winfield Scott."

"Can't I ever stump you?"

"Yep. You've stumped me right now. What's going on in that pretty head of yours, Sarah Jane? Am I the hero or the villain?"

"I— How's your mother doing?"

"Great. She loves the real-estate business. You were dead right about that, Sarah."

"Oh. I suppose you're spending a lot of time guiding her, making sure everything goes well."

"No, she doesn't seem to need it. Just this week she asked for more administrative responsibilities."

"And will you delegate some to her?"

"I'm working on it."

"Oh."

Cliff guided the horse between two parked cars and reined him to a stop at Sarah's front stoop. "We're here. Let's go in." He jumped from the saddle and helped Sarah down.

"This is ridiculous. You can't leave a horse out here."

"I imagine your landlord would prefer him out here to in your living room. Look, I can tie him to your front porch. What I have to say needs privacy, Sarah. Unlock the door, please."

Eyeing the tethered horse dubiously, she took the key from her pocket and opened the door to her apartment. Cliff followed her in, took off his cap and tossed it on a chair.

"Now," he said, grasping her by the shoulders, "I have to know if you still care about me at all, if you came to the park today out of idle curiosity or because..."

The cold chunk of misery that had been lodged inside her heart for weeks melted under the warmth of his gaze. She couldn't play games any longer. "Because I still love you," she whispered.

"Oh, Sarah." He drew her into his arms and claimed her mouth with a tremulous sigh.

Joyously she answered the passion in his kiss, parting her lips and welcoming the thrust of his tongue. She wrapped her arms around him and pressed her body tight against the brass buttons of his jacket. God, it was good to hold him again.

At last he released her and gazed into her flushed face. "Do you believe I didn't bring my mother into the business just to please you? Because I didn't. In fact, at the time I suggested the job to her, I'd vowed never to see you again."

"So I heard."

"Maureen, I bet."

"Yes, but she also said you'd changed your mind, according to some drunken confidences to Pat last night."

"Everything Pat heard—and I was not drunk, by the way—was true. I changed my mind weeks ago but figured either you had to call me or I had to wait longer before contacting you. I didn't want to blow it, Sarah."

"Has your mother agreed to take over the business eventually so you can go back to history?"

"Yes, but I'm not going back right away, Sarah."

She grew rigid in his arms. "Why not?"

"Don't get all huffy. We can't afford it just yet. Not if we're getting married, and you're going to school."

"Wait a minute. You're not putting me through school, and as for getting married—"

"Sarah, hold it."

"But—"

He gave her a little shake. "Hold it, Sarah! My God, you can be difficult. Listen to me. I've stood by while you spent your college fund on your parents' land. I'm trying to change my whole attitude about protecting the women I love. Can't you bend a little?"

"I don't want you slaving away at a job you don't like so that I can go to school."

"The job's not that bad. I don't ever intend to give up my real-estate license completely. Why throw away a chance for extra money? My dad was right about one thing—I don't want to be a pauper. Let's have the best of both worlds, Sarah. First you'll get your bachelor's, and then we'll go to graduate school together part-time."

"If we go to school part-time, you'll sell real estate, but what will I do?"

He worked the rubber band from the end of her braided hair. "We'll consider that when we get there. Maybe you'll want to go back to the hospital part-time, or who knows? Maybe you're good at selling real estate."

He unwound her braid and ran his fingers through the copper waves cascading over her shoulders. "Would you like that?" he said softly, gazing into the brown velvet of her eyes.

"Cliff...it all seems so simple."

"That's because it is simple, my darling Sarah. Don't make it complicated by trying to balance the scales exactly. Let love do that."

She searched his face, wanting to believe him but still afraid.

"Sarah, have you ever felt like this about another human being?"

She shook her head.

"Neither have I. We belong together. We always have. Ten years ago we almost lost each other, but luck brought us into each other's lives again. That first day I asked you to stay for old times' sake. Now I'm asking for the sake of all the times ahead—for a lifetime, Sarah."

At last the doubts were gone, and her radiant smile gave her decision more eloquently than words. Cliff's exultant laughter filled the small living room as he swept her into his arms and carried her to the bedroom.

"How do you feel about men in uniform?" he whispered against her ear.

"I'm a real sucker for men in uniform."

"Glad to hear it." He set her on her feet next to the bed.

"But," she added, undoing the first of his brass buttons, "there's something about a man out of uniform, too."

"I won't lose my romantic appeal?"

Sarah pushed the jacket aside and unfastened the wooden buttons on the cotton shirt underneath. "I don't think so," she said breathlessly, caressing his broad chest. "But why don't you take off all of it and we'll find out for sure?" She nudged off her shoes and lay back on the bed.

"Sounds like an excellent experiment," he replied,

reaching for his belt buckle. When he stood before her, naked and fully aroused, he lifted one eyebrow. "Well?"

Sarah held out her arms. "Come closer. I can't tell when you're so far away."

With a groan of desire, he stretched out next to her and slid his hands under her cotton blouse. "Enough games, Sarah. Let's get rid of these things."

She obliged willingly, wriggling out of her clothes as he unfastened them.

"I've missed you so much," he murmured, kissing her breasts, her stomach, her thighs. "I drove myself crazy wondering if you'd find someone else before the time was right to call you again."

She arched toward him, her hands roaming feverishly over his body. "Silly man. After loving you, I couldn't look at anyone else. Oh—there...yes, yes!"

"I love you, Sarah Jane." He moved above her and, grasping her writhing hips, buried himself deep inside her softness. For both of them the aching loneliness was over at last.

Outside Sarah's front door the horse pricked his ears at the soft cries coming from inside the apartment. He shifted his feet restlessly and gazed at the closed door. Then all was quiet, and he resumed munching on the bush beside the porch.

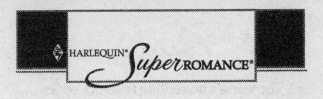

...there's more to the story!

Superromance.
A *big* satisfying read about unforgettable
characters. Each month we offer *six* very different
stories that range from family drama to adventure
and mystery, from highly emotional stories to
romantic comedies—and much more! Stories
about people you'll believe in and care about.
Stories too compelling to put down....

Our authors are among today's *best* romance
writers. You'll find familiar names and talented
newcomers. Many of them are award winners—
and you'll see why!

If you want the biggest and best
in romance fiction, you'll get it
from Superromance!

Emotional, Exciting, Unexpected...

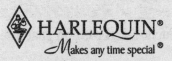

HARLEQUIN®
Makes any time special ®